POETRY MATTERS

Edited by Claire Tupholme

The West Midlands & The North Of England

First published in Great Britain in 2011 by:

Young Writers
Remus House
Coltsfoot Drive
Peterborough
PE2 9BF
Telephone: 01733 890066
Website: www.youngwriters.co.uk

Book Design by Samantha Wood

SB ISBN 978-0-85739-278-7

Foreword

Since our inception in 1991, Young Writers has endeavoured to promote poetry and creative writing within schools by running annual nationwide competitions. These competitions are designed to develop and nurture the burgeoning creativity of the next generation, and give them valuable confidence in their own abilities.

This regional anthology is one of the series produced by our latest secondary school competition, *Poetry Matters*. Using poetry as their tool, the young writers were given the opportunity to tell the world what matters to them. The authors of our favourite three poems were also given the chance to appear on the front cover of their region's collection.

Whilst skilfully conveying their opinions through poetry, the writers showcased in this collection have simultaneously managed to give poetry a breath of fresh air, brought it to life and made it relevant to them. Using a variety of themes and styles, our featured poets leave a lasting impression of their inner thoughts and feelings, making this anthology a rare insight into the next generation.

Contents

Caludon Castle School, Wyken

Caitlin Leigh (11) 1
Beth Finlan (11) 2
Kyra Donegan (11) 2
Danielle King (11) 3
Shannon Rosamond (11) 3
Rhys Phillips (11) 4
Jedd Callaghan (11) 4
Bethany Holgate (11) 5
Sofia Borras-McCrorey (12) 5
Kye Burgess (11) 6
Lucy Killestein (11) 6
Olivia Whitehouse (11) 7
Harry Powell (11) 7
Joseph Gilkes (11) 8
Regan Gavin (11) 8
Lucy Malpass (11) 9
Teri Lea Dudley (12) 9
Taylor Gilder (11) 10
Emily Single (11) 10

Etone College, Nuneaton

Bernice Cherian (12) 11
Charlie Hartley (11) 12
Matt Fisher (12) 13
Ryan Boneham (12) 13
Chloe Ferguson (11) 14
Bethany Mountford (11) 15
Michael Irvine (11) 15
Mariam Mahmood (13) 16
Parris Grant (11) 17
Saalihah Bilimoria (13) 18
Lucy Parlett (14) 19
Megan Drew (11) 20
Matthew Cartwright (11) 21
Ashley-Thomas Jones (13) 22
Nabeela Pathan (11) 22
Alanna Masters (12) 23
Iona Lusty (12) 23
Kaneeze Akil (13) 24
Gemma Cartern (12) 24
Gabriella Gwyer Jones (13) 25
Danny Skaric (12) 25
Rebecca Cave (13) 26
Kerry Daffern (11) 26
Katie Paget (13) 27
Jack Barlow (13) 27
Naomi Taylor (13) 28
Emily Grimstead (11) 29
Jameel Malik (12) 29
Scarlett Dearing (11) 30
Aimee Iverson (11) 30
Sophie Ross (11) 31
Luke Randle (13) 31
Tasneem Mulla (11) 32
Thomas Painter (11) 32
Ahmed Fatuwala (13) 33
Kimberley Swan (13) 33
Lucy Fensome (13) 34
Paris Notman (11) 34
Sanjay Patel (13) 35
Tess Cave (11) 35
Sandip Gurung (11) 36
Poppy Louise Groves (12) 36
Robbie Barnes (12) 37
Farhah Din (13) 37
Kelsey Betteridge (12) 38
Bethany Adler-Smith (13) 38
Jamie Downs (13) 39
Quddoosiyyah Esmail (13) 39
Mark Parlett (11) 40
Chelsea Parker (12) 40

Lucee Read (12) 41
Lewis Humphriss (11) 41
Dylan Ogilvie (12) 42
Courtney Gould (12) 42
Georgie Bedford (12) 43
Musa Karolia (11) 43
Emily Bell (11) 44
Rumana Sheikh (12) 44
Ryan Lucas (12) 45
Lucy Price (13) 45
David Manns (12) 46
Kirstie Penn (13) 46
Jessica Peat (14) 47
Zaki Bhaiyat (11) 47
Ceara Evans (11) 48
Taylor Charnell (11) 48
Eliot Phillips (11) 49
Michael Adams (11) 49
Briony Harris (11) 50
Thomas Costall (12) 50
Jack Neale (11) 51
Felicity Dodson (12) 51
Luke Perrohn (12) 52
Kieran Folan (11) 52
Caitlin Watson (12) 53
Joe Smith (11) 53
Aliyah Patel (11) 54
Fraser Powell (11) 54
Cory Richardson (14) 54
Ieuan Llewellyn (13) 55
Kirsty Folan (13) 55
Grace Greenaway (12) 55
Sophia Evans (11) 56
Callum Cheshire (13) 56
Jack Bannister (11) 56
Rosie Parsons (13) 57
Jacob Lloyd (11) 57
Jessica Bate (13) 57

St James' CE Secondary School, Farnworth

Jennifer Walton (15) 58
Ryan Kitchen (11) 60
Roshni Dhodakia (12) 61
Ellie Cook (11) 61
Molly Costello (11) 62
Lauren Tonge (12) 63
Luke Williams (11) 63
Alannah Pierce-Jackson (11) 63
Idnan Ahmed (12) 64
Harvey Townsend (11) 64
Aqil Chachia (12) 65
Arif Bham (11) 65
George Miller (12) 66
Amelia Thomas (12) 66
Muhammad Adia (12) 77
Shivam Patel (11) 77
Yameen Mallu (12) 78
Burnden Lee Horrocks (12) 78
Samantha Young (12) 79
James Lord (12) 79
Binisha Harivadan Vekaria (12) 80
Haroon Parvez (11) 80
Hasan Patel (11) 81
Dhillon Lad (12) 81
Ammarah Rawat (12) 82
Rudra Dave (12) 82
Callum Foster (11) 83
Akash Gujjar (11) 83
Zain Ahmed (12) 84
Libby Cowburn (12) 84
Rebekah Coghlin (11) 85
Rutendo Dhandinda (12) 85
Ismail Adia (13) 86
Niall Airey (12) 86
Faisal Kaduji (12) 87
Nicole Tyler (13) 87
Joshua John Thompson (11) 88

Tejal Rana (11) 88
Amir Kala (11) 89
Chris Galley (11) 89
Holly Ghoorun (11) 90
Nisha Patel (11) 90
Jessica Furness (11) 91
Neve Rosevere (12) 91
Usamah Khan (11) 92
Nadiya Patel (12) 92
Rebecca Tracey (13) 93
Aimée Parmar (12) 93
Robert Leyland (12) 94
Jessica Yates (12) 94
Jamie Whittle (12) 95
Rebecca Walker (12) 95
Rebecca Rose Preston (12) 96
Zaini Miraj (12) 96
Krishan Tailor (12) 97
Jakub Amin (11) 97
Louie Halliwell (11) 97
Sophie Middleton (12) 98
Ben Fennell (12) 98
Taybah Hassan (12) 99
Luke Thurston (12) 99
Helen Sulkey (12) 100
Firdose Valli (12) 100
Dhylan Jadwa (12) 101
Rayan Saleh (12) 101
Jasmine Patel (11) 102
Holly Leece (11) 102
Robyn Boyden (11) 102
Bradley Thorpe (11) 103
Jade Hayden (11) 103
Aidan Smith (11) 103
Ryan Newman (11) 104
Abdul Aleem (11) 104
Vishaal Parmar (11) 105
Megan Brooks (11) 105
Alireza Mafie (13) 106
Ellise Gillard (12) 106
Adam Walker (12) 107
Anita Vekaira (11) 107
Lisa Banks (12) 107
Patrick Kelly (12) 108
Joshua Worswick (12) 108
Mitul Pankhania (12) 109
Chloe Fairclough (12) 109
Aaron Robinson (12) 109
Hamza Rana (11) 110
Brandon Topp (12) 110
Daniel Worthington (11) 110
Abigail Heywood (11) 111
Dhruv Chevli (11) 111
Matthew Cottam 111
Bilaal Khan (11) 112
Emilia Singh (11) 112
Alisha Bond (11) 112
Ahmed Chohan (11) 113
Zahra Khan (11) 113
Charlotte Turner (11) 113
Chris German (11) 113
Rachel Hayes (11) 114
Jacob Swaries (12) 114
Sameer Patel (11) 114
Uvais Malji (11) 114
Daniel Hulmes (12) 115
Husain Patel (11) 115
Corben Davies (11) 115
Unaisah Patel (11) 115
Corben John Davies (11) 116
Jamil Noorgat (11) 116
Jake Taylor (11) 116
Victoria Unwin (11) 116

Summerhill Secondary School, Kingswinford

Abigail Blood (11) 117

The Queen's School, Chester

Matilda Lloyd Williams (12).. 118
Jessica Reed (13).. 119
Bethany Reed (13).. 120

Upton Hall School, Wirral

Claire Lightfoot.. 121
Stephanie Addenbrooke (15).. 122
Rebecca Airey.. 123
Amy Naylor.. 124

Westleigh High School, Leigh

Lewis Bolton (12).. 124
Ashley Poole (14).. 125
Georgia Fishburn (13).. 126
Barney Warburton (13).. 127
Nathan Murray (13).. 128
Alicia Lovely (13).. 129
Chelsea Latter (14).. 130
Charlotte Durham (13).. 131
Nathan Pittendrigh (12).. 131
Hayley Masheder (13).. 132
Sophie Bretherton (13).. 132
Adam Cachia (13).. 133
Abbie O'Neil (12).. 133
Callum Barber (12).. 134
Rachel Alice Gregory (12).. 134
Connor Sharratt (13).. 135
Joy Burns (13).. 136
Rebecca Cotterell (12).. 137
Dillon Swanton (14).. 138
Jordan Hellam (12).. 138
Lewis Grimes (12).. 139

The Poems

Chocolate

Melting, soft, luxurious candy
Just don't drop it in Coke
And never make it sandy
And don't keep giving it a poke

Chocolate is enough to make you sick
But it never tires you
And is easy to pick
You and your friends can enjoy it too

It only costs you £1 a day
And it's so scrumptious
It's not much to pay
And it's delicious

It's only a thick paste
And it's hardened
It doesn't go to waste
You might need to be pardoned

Don't suck your fingers, after they will be sour
But the best is Cadbury's
It's only one pour
Just don't change it to Mad-bury.

Chocolate is the best
Chocolate isn't a pest
Chocolate is the world
Long live chocolate.

Caitlin Leigh (11)
Caludon Castle School, Wyken

Everything I Love

I love all of my books
because when I'm bored I start to read one.
I love my CD player
because it plays my favourite songs.
I love my Nintendo DS
because it makes me feel happy.
I love my mobile
because I can contact people.
I love my posters on the wall
because they decorate my bedroom.
I love my jewellery
I love my rubbers
I love my bouncy ball
I love my family
I love my friends
I love everything that belongs to me.

Beth Finlan (11)
Caludon Castle School, Wyken

My Dog, Izzy

My dog Izzy,
Is as fluffy as a cloud
And she is my best friend.

She licks me,
She jumps at me
And she also plays with me.

She's afraid of cats,
She doesn't like birds,
But of course she likes me.

I love her,
She loves me,
My dog is the best dog in the world!

Kyra Donegan (11)
Caludon Castle School, Wyken

Friends

(People who are always there for you)

F riends are people who at times you may hate,
but are great,
R easonable and loving,
whether you're crying or blubbering,
I n sticky situations they are the people who are always there,
when you need a little extra care,
E verlasting friendships are ones that matter most,
when you're really close,
N ever alone when you have a pal,
who your secrets you can tell,
D iscussing things you wouldn't tell anyone else,
as if you're in your own secret house,
S ecrets are things that keep you close,
but friendship always matters most.

Danielle King (11)
Caludon Castle School, Wyken

My Dad!

My dad is special to me,
He is like a big cuddly bear,
When I hug him every day.
I love the way he talks and laughs and plays, and jokes,
But most of all I love the way it always hurts my throat.

He always gets poorer and poorer every day,
But soon we'll have a big new house
And we will be saying hip hip *hooray!*

My dad's name is Hollis,
And he means the world to me,
But when he's gone, I don't know who I'll be.

I love you Dad!

Shannon Rosamond (11)
Caludon Castle School, Wyken

My Family

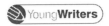

My family is the most significant to me,
On Earth no one will be able to see.
I love you *so, so* much,
Like you would know, as such.
Nothing will ever be able to compare,
Not even the cuddliest teddy bear.
I love you more than you will know,
No one ever needs to ask are they friend or foe.
Mum, Dad and Lauren, you're the best,
By miles far better than the rest.
You are what keeps me breathing every day,
I don't know what I'll do when you pass away!

Thank you
I love you.

Rhys Phillips (11)
Caludon Castle School, Wyken

Poetry

P oetry is great for rhyming, also is a skill
O bedience is needed when you are stuck
E den Falls water is great when you need to chill
T alk to yourself, tell yourself you need a bit of luck
R eading is cool when you make a mistake
Y ou are the poet, so show it!

Jedd Callaghan (11)
Caludon Castle School, Wyken

My Sister, Chelsea

My sister Chelsea
Is very, very kind,
She's in sixth form
And she doesn't mind.
Being in sixth form is a lot of work,
But she gets on with it so it doesn't hurt.

My sister Chelsea
Is a bit of a bore,
She used to be funny
But not anymore.

My sister Chelsea
Is like a bin,
She eats everything
Although she is really thin.

Bethany Holgate (11)
Caludon Castle School, Wyken

Winter Day

Snowmen wave in white sky,
Children make snow angels,
A white blanket covers the rooftops,
Icicles hang under the cars,
Snowflakes giggle as they fall,
The sky is full with cotton wool,
A wintry day has gone!

Sofia Borras-McCrorey (12)
Caludon Castle School, Wyken

My Dog - KC

I had my dog when I was nine
It's like she was meant to be mine
I love my dog
More than a frog
She's so cuddly
Like a soft teddy bear
When I come in from school
She licks me like a fool
She's the best dog in the world!
If you don't love dogs you've got to be mad
I love dogs more than a zoo
I love dogs . . .
How about you?

Kye Burgess (11)
Caludon Castle School, Wyken

Rabbits

Rabbits are fun,
And are able hiders.
They love to run,
And are fast like spiders.

Rabbits are rather grumpy at times,
But also big fusspots.
They are also complete troublemakers,
Rabbits eat everything in your plant pots.

My rabbit loves his nibble sticks made with honey,
He chomps them up and you can almost hear him say yummy.
Scampy is his name and he really is quite funny,
Oh how I love my bunny.

Lucy Killestein (11)
Caludon Castle School, Wyken

A Little Fish In A Great Big Pool

I'm a little fish in a great big pool,
I'm a Year 7 in a brand new school,
I've got new friends and new teachers too,
I got lost at lunch and crushed in the queue.

I make my way around this huge place,
I check my timetable, I need a friendly face,
I can hear footsteps charging up the hall,
Oh no it's Year 10s, I hang on to the wall.

My new teachers are helpful and some are good fun,
My new blazer is baggy and my bag weighs a tonne!
I need to study hard and still be cool,
I'm such a little fish in a great big pool!

Olivia Whitehouse (11)
Caludon Castle School, Wyken

My Mum

My mum is special
She is perfect
Her smile is as bright as the sparkling moon
She means the world to me!

Mum gives me the best of things
The happy attitude she has makes my day
She works really hard to care for me
But her silly jokes always make me laugh

Her heart is as precious as gold!
And is as big as the universe!
She is the best mentor
Mum, you're the best!

Harry Powell (11)
Caludon Castle School, Wyken

A Witch's Poem

'Double, double toil and trouble,
Fire burn and cauldron bubble.'
A handful of frog spawn,
The sharpest point of a goat's horn,
Five curly monkey's tails,
One hundred slimy, slippery snails,
Owl's claw, eyeball of dog,
Cat's paw, snout of hog,
Eight spider's legs, an oyster's shell,
All mixed together for an evil spell.
'Double, double toil and trouble
Fire burn and cauldron bubble'.

Joseph Gilkes (11)
Caludon Castle School, Wyken

Horrible Potion

20 frogs' legs
3 metal pegs
6ml of shampoo
20kg of cows' poo

3 cans of honey
7 tails of a bunny
12 eyes of a spider
1 can of smoke to make milder

That's the witch's potion
Be careful of the motion.

Regan Gavin (11)
Caludon Castle School, Wyken

My Sister, Laura

My sister, Laura,
Can be quite mean,
She likes doing gardening
And she's quite keen!

She changes like the weather,
She's like a chameleon,
I know she's not,
But she thinks she's a comedian.

I know she's my sister and I love her lots . . .
I've always thought, that's she's a spoilsport.

Lucy Malpass (11)
Caludon Castle School, Wyken

The Witches' Spell

(Based on 'The Witches' Spell' from Macbeth)

Three witches with a spell to make,
Which ingredients shall they bake?
The slime of a slug and toe of a frog.
Eye of a snake and tail of a dog.
An ear of a rabbit and a wasp's sting.
The leg of a spider and a pigeon's wing.
'Double, double toil and trouble,
Fire burn and cauldron bubble'.

Teri Lea Dudley (12)
Caludon Castle School, Wyken

The Morning

I wake up to a buzz
Rub my eyes and ignore the fuss.
The shout follows not once but twice
Please go away, I need my sleep.
Thud, thud, thud, I hear the stairs
This must be Mum, I'd best prepare.
Do I hide or jump straight up?
Can't wait for the weekend
I can get a lie in.

Taylor Gilder (11)
Caludon Castle School, Wyken

Spirit Of Coventry

It makes me feel very special,
My marching band is fab,
It's the best feeling ever when you win!
The flag is like a bright colourful rainbow
Floating in the warm sunny air, amidst the beautiful music.
The rifles are a huge heavy gun spinning, throwing, catching
And twirling.
Our aim is to win the tall trophy that sparkles and shines.

Emily Single (11)
Caludon Castle School, Wyken

My Fortune Home

A house is made out of bricks,
With all the cement mixed,
People with relationships,
Make a house a home,

Home is a place of freedom,
A freedom that I live all through my life,
Feeling safe all day and night,
Happiness at day and warmth at night,

A house full of bright colours,
Still dull ones come through,
But the bright one doesn't let it show,
With a big smile that never lets go,

A house full of flowers
With the fragrance dispersing rapidly,
Spreading the smell of emotions
From the floor to the ceiling,

A fortune given by God,
By showing kindness to me,
That some children dream for
24/7 of their life.
This is what matters to me.

Bernice Cherian (12)
Etone College, Nuneaton

When Will It End?

When will it end the cutting down of trees?
Bringing rainforest animals to their knees.

When will it end the chaos in Africa,
Now listen 'cause I'm tellin' ya,
There's a problem in that area,
Because everyone's dying of malaria.
And did you know about the horror,
That they're getting ill and dying,
'Cause there is no clean water.

And if I'm honest I'd be kissin' ya,
If you helped solve the problems in India,
Every day a little boy's working,
Breaking a bone and losing a limb
Just to try and earn a living.
All the children are suffering from confusion,
There are girls nine and ten
Who have to make ends meet through prostitution.

Now I'll talk about pandas,
They are dying out but we've got the power,
To save them all but we've got to act now.

Then an orang-utan dies
'Cause someone wants some palm oil found in palm trees.
Why can't you see,
We are taking down their trees on their own soil.

Now there are donkeys who are working every day,
They're working in the boiling sun by the way.

They are getting no rests, no water, no shade,
But their poor owner can't come to their aid.

They are getting bad backs because they're carrying sacks,
Filled with tons of bricks, what a shame.

Now I'm beggin' you please,
Because they keep falling on their knees,
They're dying on the floor but their owner can do nothing
But we can do something.

Tigers, leopards and so many more,
Are being driven to extinction so I have been thinkin',
I can do something about it so can you all.

Cats, dogs are being beaten,
But we can make a difference,
We can save them.

Please help the world we live in,
'Cause between you and me
So far as I can see,
I'm an 11-year-old boy
And this is really what matters to me.

Charlie Hartley (11)
Etone College, Nuneaton

History

History is a mystery to us all
We don't know who put it there at all
That is why we study it at school
So that is why
History is a mystery to all.

Matt Fisher (12)
Etone College, Nuneaton

Oil Leak

O n the riverbed lies an enemy.
I t goes with the wars and pollution.
L ike a black demon in the mist.

L ike a shape that invades the sea.
E veryone who takes it on will lose.
A ll mankind can't stop it
K illing and things that swim in it.

Ryan Boneham (12)
Etone College, Nuneaton

What Matters To Me Is Food!

I love food
But not any food
This food
Chips
Dips
Licky lips
Bubblegum
Drink some rum
Have some fun
Chicken's done
Lollipops
In the shops
For 5 or 10p
Cup of tea
I've eaten curry happily
For my lunch
Or for my tea
I don't mind, it's just curry
I'm in a hurry
To eat my lunch
I might have crisps
Or
A Munch Bunch
I like pizza
With a spicy topping
I look out the window at a rabbit hopping
I love breakfast
Lunch and
Dinner
If I don't eat
I will get thinner
For breakfast I like toast with jam
For lunch I like a sandwich with ham
For dinner I like anything but lamb.

Chloe Ferguson (11)
Etone College, Nuneaton

My Magic Box

(Based on 'Magic Box' by Kit Wright)

I will put in my magic box . . .
The cold winds of the autumn months,
The last leaf left on the tree,
A pinch of snow from the frost-bitten ground,
And a hot summer day.

I will put in my box . . .
The breath of an angel,
A feather slowly falling,
The delicate steps of a dancer
And a single white wish.

I will put in my box . . .
The dust blown off an ancient book,
A grain of sand from the Sahara Desert,
A bucket full of rainbow colours
And a shooting star.

The final things I will put in my box:
A birth, a death,
A smile, a tear,
A whisper.

Bethany Mountford (11)
Etone College, Nuneaton

The Storm

The dark grey bank of cloud was like an army charging
As white horses gathered to make the tide as strong as a rusty chainsaw
In the sky the lightning was as bright as the sun
And the hail was as strong as a muscle
With the rain beating as wet as the Pacific Ocean.

Michael Irvine (11)
Etone College, Nuneaton

A Beaten Life

She enjoys her life,
She enjoys her nights with her family,
She enjoys school . . .
She enjoys school until a certain lesson,
That lesson she dreads,
That lesson she fears,
That lesson she tries to avoid.

Three girls just stand there and gossip . . .
Gossip about that girl.
Saying she's ugly and saying she's fat,
They laugh and giggle, their witches' cackles echo through her ear.
Once, used to be friends, now enemies.

She turns to her best friend, who reassures her.
Her eyes full of tears and a body of pain,
Her friend full of affection and comfort,
Not letting her go insane!
After school she's relieved, but still a little depressed,
She walks home all alone
And thinks about her day.

She sits with her family for dinner,
And pretends that nothing happened at school today.

She goes to her room and puts on her favourite music,
Then talks to her friends online.
Just then that spiteful girl comes online
And posts this girl a hurtful message . . .
Just then, a flashback comes to her head
Of slaps and punches, kicks and the pulls of hair.
It haunts her every day and every night.
She stares at the bruises upon her arm just for a little while.
She gets ready for bed and lies down,
She cuddles her teddy and thinks about her day
With tears in her eyes, she quietly weeps herself to sleep . . .

Mariam Mahmood (13)
Etone College, Nuneaton

The Graveyard

I like the graveyard,
It's cold and cruel,
The atmosphere is dense and dark,
People mourn,
People cry,
I sit and listen to what they say,
Every night and every day,
They don't know I'm there but I really am,
I like the graveyard.

I sit on the cold, neglected ground,
Making little mud mounds,
People sigh,
People moan,
They ruin my little mud mounds,
Sometimes I cry,
Sometimes I sigh,
I like the graveyard.

My family comes every year,
Mourn and cry as everyone does,
I go up to them and try to feel their warm skin,
They shiver,
My hand goes right through them,
I like the graveyard because . . .
It's my home and has been for twelve years,

I'm not like everyone else,
I'm a ghost and nothing else.

Parris Grant (11)
Etone College, Nuneaton

Closing My Eyes

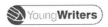

Morning!
the sun shines in through the window,
sweet song of happy birds,
is heard.

Laughter drives in through
the open window,
I go down the colourful landing
and get greeted with bright smiles . . .

The day has gone,
happy thoughts stream into my mind
smiling, I finally shut my eyes
and go to sleep.

Bang! Go, go, go!
I wake up with a jolt,
the day is dark,
cries of people are heard.
The screaming siren rings,
now I jump out of bed.
I run down the dull landing,
running for shelter
I duck, *bang!*

Closing my eyes I hear
the final cries of plea.

Saalihah Bilimoria (13)
Etone College, Nuneaton

I Have A Power

I have a power,
That everyone in my country shares,
I have the power to speak freely.

I have a power,
That everyone in my country shares,
I have the power to walk freely.

I have a power,
That allows me to end all wars,
I have the power to be in control.

I have a power,
That allows me to heal all people,
I have the power to be in control.

I have a power,
That lets me stop disasters,
I have the power to say stop right there.

I have a power,
That lets me stop disasters,
I have the power to rescue innocent lives.

I have a power,
You have a power,
We have a power,
So we can all make a difference.

Lucy Parlett (14)
Etone College, Nuneaton

My Rainbow

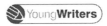

When the sun embarks to hide,
And the damp meadows mellow.
I see my rainbow.

The infernal desperation to embrace its radiation,
Pulls at me,
Tugs at me,
I could never be that patient,
But then I see my rainbow.

It hears the tear in my soul,
Replenishing me with true tranquillity,
I thank my rainbow.

My arms reach out to it,
Begging for its freedom
I need my rainbow.

I let out a Hell-like scream,
Could this tepid beauty be real?
Is it just a maddening dream?

I pray for its glance,
Pleading for it to truly enhance,
That he is my rainbow.

Megan Drew (11)
Etone College, Nuneaton

Creaking Floorboards

She gets out the car
And throws back the door,
She walks up the drive
And unlocks the porch.

But something's wrong,
The lights aren't on.
There's no one home
And the house is dead.

She steps inside,
The floorboards creak,
She looks around
And then she shrieks.

He hits her hard
Right on the head,
She lays there cold,
Sprawled on her bed.

He runs away
Scared to death.
And tonight that girl
Had her last breath.

Matthew Cartwright (11)
Etone College, Nuneaton

The Beauty Of St Ives

The golden sands of Porthminster,
Rushing through your toes.
The roar
Of the crashing blue sea.
Looking out the bedroom window . . .
Waking up to seagulls.
Go surfing,
Enjoy the high waves of Porthmear.
Hundreds of surfers,
Body boarders,
Learners too.
It's now time for lunch,
We head up to the Sheaf of Wheat,
The carvery is unbeatable.
And it's only cheap.
Now we have had our dinner,
We get some drinks and listen to the karaoke.
The sun starts heading down,
We start heading up the hill until we arrive at our guest house.
I run up to my room,
Slip on my pjs
And run downstairs to talk to my mate.

Ashley-Thomas Jones (13)
Etone College, Nuneaton

What Matters To Me!

What matters to me is my family,
My mum has love,
My brother says, 'Brov,'
My sister is so cute
While the other is playing the lute.
My dad dancing happily,
What matters to me is my family.

Nabeela Pathan (11)
Etone College, Nuneaton

Frog Poem

Sitting on a log,
I see a frog!

A big-eyed beauty,
What a cutey!

I am so keen,
As it's gorgeous and green!

It catches a fly,
As it goes by!

It has a bright red tongue,
That is curled and long!

Through my ear,
A cute *ribbit* is what I hear!

As I see it hop,
My heart fills a lot!

From dwarf frogs,
To claw frogs!

Many types that I see,
I realise how much they matter to me!

Alanna Masters (12)
Etone College, Nuneaton

The World

I love the flowers and the trees,
The bushes and the breeze,
It means everything to me.
I love the colours of the rainbow,
The red, pink and green,
It makes me feel like the Queen.
All the beauty that I see,
Means everything to me.

Iona Lusty (12)
Etone College, Nuneaton

Nothing . . . !

My mind stays empty,
I don't know what to write,
Should it be about mountains,
Squirrels, cats or mice?

My head stays blank,
I cannot think,
The birds start singing,
Ugh, think, think, *think!*

I get too many distractions,
The sun is in my face,
I can't concentrate,
Due to the guy sitting next to me,
He is a big disgrace.

I keep on thinking,
And a few minutes later I say,
Wait a minute,
I can write about something,
I know what to call it,
Nothing . . . !

Kaneeze Akil (13)
Etone College, Nuneaton

Sisters

Some sisters argue,
Some may fight,
But my sister doesn't,
She gives me the most advice.

Sometimes they don't care,
And never have the time,
But mine has the heart,
To love me all the time.

Gemma Cartern (12)
Etone College, Nuneaton

Elegance

Hoisting myself up into the saddle,
while he stands patiently waiting,
his head tucked in,
looking pretty.

With a squeeze of my heels,
we're off,
in a nice bouncy trot,
paced and elevated,
as bouncy as a ping-pong ball.

Lowering my head and checking my diagonal sitting,
going into a three beat canter,
as smooth as a baby's bum.

Looking down the centre line,
turning,
keeping my leg on till I get to X,
X and I squeeze my reigns,
halting,
saluting,
finished.

Gabriella Gwyer Jones (13)
Etone College, Nuneaton

My Brothers

I wake up to a sight
See my brother and I'm in for a fright
Jumping here and there
Trying to wake me but I don't care
Rolling, turning, trying not to wake
Then my little brother jumps on my face
I get up angrily, throw him off
Then I go back to bed, finish it off
In the end it's only a game.

Danny Skaric (12)
Etone College, Nuneaton

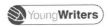

What Is Freedom?

Freedom is the ability to do what you want.
To feel how you want to feel.
To have your own opinions.

It is something people often take for granted;
But for people who don't have it, it's something they long for.
Some people will risk their lives for it;
Others will just sit back and watch.

Just imagine what it would be like,
Having no choice,
No feelings,
No opinions,
No nothing.

Are you making the most of your freedom?
Voting,
Saying your opinions,
Showing emotions,
Being who you want to be.

This is what matters to me.

Rebecca Cave (13)
Etone College, Nuneaton

My Family

What matters to me is my family.
My mum, you know she's always there,
Especially if I start to get scared.
My dad helps me all the time,
So if I'm stuck, I will be fine.
My brothers and sisters stick up for me
And I'm never lonely as you can see.
I have a big family, so I feel safe,
All my family give me faith!

Kerry Daffern (11)
Etone College, Nuneaton

Zombie Poem

The undead horde
Stagger towards me
Ha, no match
For my automatic shotgun
Head shot
Blood and fractions of rotting
Brain explodes
Across the floor
A child
Crouched in a ball
On the floor
Sobbing
The freaks
Astound towards me
And the child
Open fire, rapidly
We're safe . . .

. . . for now.

Katie Paget (13)
Etone College, Nuneaton

The Sparrow

The sparrow is a little bird,
That everyone can love,
Even more than any lovely dove.
And we see them everywhere,
More than a rabbit or a hare.
They are common in our land,
We all think the sparrow is grand.
And that is all I wish to say,
Off I go,
Good day.

Jack Barlow (13)
Etone College, Nuneaton

A Snowy Christmas!

On Christmas Eve you can't sleep,
With imagination gone wild,
'What did Santa get me?' little children cry.

On the morning of Christmas,
He gazes out his window,
A blanket of snow covers the streets,
Like cotton wool has fallen in the night!
Whoosh! Whoosh! Whoosh! as the children go by,
On ice skates gliding on a sheet of glass.

'Mum, Dad, Santa's eaten my cookies and has drunk my milk. He's been! He's been!'

He runs to the living room,
With hope and excitement,
He rips his presents,
Like a Tazmanian devil.
'Yay!' he shouts as he sees his toys,
'Just what I wanted.'

Another Christmas success.

Naomi Taylor (13)
Etone College, Nuneaton

The Dream Of Blue

Glimmering on the peaks of the horizon
Shimmering turquoise blue sheet blankets the creatures of the deep
Swaying from side to side like a tree saying hello
Rocking the Earth to sleep - cradling their worries away
Calm and quiet the golden pathway oozes between my feet
Emerald-like hair trailing through the deep blue
No wailing screech to be seen or heard
The iceberg of salt takes a stroll of trepidation around my taste buds
A delicate touch of the water's surface - a tingling chill
My heart is the world, the sea is my dream . . .

Emily Grimstead (11)
Etone College, Nuneaton

An Insignificant War

As we gaze at a fiery bullet's flood,
We lie in trenches full of blood,
Sitting under a fire-like sky.
As the sun sets into the water of Normandy beach,
The water is lit like fire . . .
Raging . . . raging closer,
But will it bring what we desire.
A vessel of hope,
Or a vessel of despair.
If that we wouldn't care
Till then we lie in agony and despair.

Jameel Malik (12)
Etone College, Nuneaton

Who Am I?

My fluffy fur is like a blanket of golden silk,
I wave my shimmering tail over my classic bowl of milk,
When I walk, I walk with pride,
And I hate it when I have this dog by my side.

My paws are pale pink and feel like leather,
I have a great name
And no it's not Trevor
I have a sandpaper tongue
And I love to sing a happy song.

I'm not as pretty as a daisy,
And to be honest I am sort of lazy,
I have precious golden fur,
And I never say please or thank you Sir.

I love to eat, I'm kind of fat,
And yes you're right,
I am a cat,
I am Garfield!

Scarlett Dearing (11)
Etone College, Nuneaton

Sea Shine

The sounds of seagulls fill the air,
I look around everywhere.
I make sandcastles . . . 1 . . . 2 . . . 3
Maybe you could help me?
The sea is waving at the sand,
I can't see any dry land.
Seashell collecting, off I go,
My bucket's full, oh no!
The day's passed, I don't know how,
I'm sorry but it's time to go now.

Aimee Iverson (11)
Etone College, Nuneaton

My Life, My Personality

I always have to be nice and warm,
And I love being cosy in a dorm.
I am very good at running,
But I'm also sort of cunning.

I am an only child,
So I am very wild.
I like to ice skate,
And I don't like to wait.

I am very funny,
And I don't like to spend money.
I like food,
And I always change my mood.

I like to read,
But I'm not a good lead.
I like talking,
But I absolutely love walking.

Sophie Ross (11)
Etone College, Nuneaton

Everything

I have no top ten because with me everything is equal
There is no sequel
My family, my friends, my dog is a bulldog
My dog is my number one friend
On that you can depend
He wakes me in the morning
And he is the last person I see at night-time
Sometimes the world is silent to me
But the landscape looks good to me

With a sense of charity
Everything is good with me.

Luke Randle (13)
Etone College, Nuneaton

All About Me

I am as beautiful as a rose,
Shiny as a glittering star,
Books dancing around me,
The colour purple is always with me,
And my bedroom gives me a relaxed mind.

The winter colours fading away,
Here comes the summer sky,
The clouds swimming around,
Just like a professional swimmer.

There I go in the beach
With the waves splashing onto me,
The sun going in to my eyes,
What a wonderful summer.

I rush into the shopping centre,
Pushing through many people,
As I carry my shopping bags,
I chuckle with glee.

Tasneem Mulla (11)
Etone College, Nuneaton

A Poem About Me

(Inspired by 'The Writer of this Poem' by Roger McGough)

The writer of this poem is Thomas Painter
Funny as a clown in the circus
Small as a grape in the fruit box
Brown as a door in the beauty room
Dirty as yellow teeth
Handsome as a man who is happy
Hairy as a dog running along
Clever as an owl who is flying every night
Noisy as a cow from the farm
Roaring as loud as a lion in the zoo.

Thomas Painter (11)
Etone College, Nuneaton

There Are Bombs!

Bombs are nowhere to be seen
But they're always mean.
Bombs are always loud
But never to be proud.
Bombs hurt
But blow a lot of dirt.
Bombs are mean
But create a big scene.
This is poetry
This is poetry
This is poetry.
Bombs are old
But are never to be sold.
Some die and some are injured
Some are round
Some make a big sound.
This is poetry
And they are bombs.

Ahmed Fatuwala (13)
Etone College, Nuneaton

Love

What matters to me is love
The love of nature
Friends, family, pets
Romantic scenes;
The world and more.
You love your life,
Love, it's a funny thing
You can give or receive
Enjoy or regret
But whatever you believe
You should love your life.

Kimberley Swan (13)
Etone College, Nuneaton

Heaven

Bursting
through disappointed clouds
into a beautiful
white and gold paradise
jumping from cloud to cloud
to get to your destination
being elevated up the golden escalators
through the great gold gates
descended relatives walking round
like nothing has happened
wearing white robes
golden halos
and huge, elegant, golden wings
I look down to discover I'm wearing the same
while I'm still peering down I see
a glint of sadness
I see my family grieving.

Lucy Fensome (13)
Etone College, Nuneaton

What Matters To Me!

What matters to me is food.
Not eating food is really bad,
Not eating food makes me sad,
But eating food makes me glad.

Pizza, chips, sausages and beans,
These are the foods that matter to me,
Not all those disgusting veggie greens.

What I am telling you is true,
But, I love food; how about you?

My favourite drink is a cup of tea,
These are the foods that matter to me!

Paris Notman (11)
Etone College, Nuneaton

Fun And Friends

What matters to me
Not the PS3
Or the coloured TV
Playing with my friends
Bradley and Matty

Going to the park
Playing till training
At the football field

They are like my brothers
From different mothers

From Arsenal, Chelsea and Liverpool
Comes our footy team
Badger Boys

These are the things that matter to me
Having fun and playing with my friends.

Sanjay Patel (13)
Etone College, Nuneaton

Snow

White and fluffy, floating from above,
Stepping through the blanket of snow,
Hearing it crunch beneath my feet,
Feeling the light touch of the snowflakes landing on my shoulder,
Sitting by the fire, drinking hot chocolate
And looking out of the window
To see little white people dancing in the air.

Seeing children building snowmen,
Freezing when you're outside but warm in the arms of a loved one,
Putting your woolly hat and gloves on before a snowball fight with friends,
It's better than sun and much better than rain,
It can only be snow.

Tess Cave (11)
Etone College, Nuneaton

What Matters To Me

What matters to me is my family,
My dad, the oldest one,
My mom, the caring one,
My sister, the annoying one.
My dad loves playing football as much as he loves himself.
My mom and sister love shopping, but not as much as me.
My friends are great,
They're great like my other mates,
They're always there.
I love playing killing games,
Blood coming out from anywhere,
I hope they die in peace,
Because I won't be with them anywhere.

Sandip Gurung (11)
Etone College, Nuneaton

My Brother And Sister

My brother is annoying,
Really, really annoying,
He always stays in the bath too long,
And he never looks after the pets,
He always leaves it to me and my sister,
Which is so annoying.

My sister is annoying,
So, so annoying,
She always slaps me really hard
And she snores so bad
And that is why I'm always tired
And that is annoying,
But the worst thing is they're *twins!*

Poppy Louise Groves (12)
Etone College, Nuneaton

I Am . . .

I am taller than tall,
I love it when small people get jealous
Or when other tall people are just plain rebellious.

I am smaller than small,
I love it when tall people just flap their beaks
Or when other small people are just full of cheek.

I am smarter than smart,
I love it when dumb people look so glum
Or when smart people are really just plums.

I am dumber than dumb,
I love it when smart people just fly off their go-karts
Or when dumb people just love to suck their thumbs.

I am more normal than normal,
I love it when people say I'm normal but
I hate it when people say I'm not.

Robbie Barnes (12)
Etone College, Nuneaton

Me

I'm a daughter
I'm a sarcastic sister
I'm an annoying pupil
I'm a lovely granddaughter
I'm a fashion queen
I'm a funny poser
I'm a collector of shoes
I'm a make-up artist
I'm myself
I'm someone.

Farhah Din (13)
Etone College, Nuneaton

Creation

Is it possible to be as proud as I am,
to have created this outstanding creature?
Her essence of beauty,
blows your busy head into peace!
Her unique posture is magnificently mind-blowing,
as it makes you believe something only I know,
for sure.
Even though she might sound pleasantly fantastic,
her blue icy lips even make the day feel unsafe!
Her cold frosty skin can kill with a short gaze of piercing eyes
that could shoot straight through you, even me,
the creator,
petrified!

Kelsey Betteridge (12)
Etone College, Nuneaton

Just For One Day . . .

For one day . . .
I wish the world would stop,
The armed forces to stop,
The fighting to stop!

For one day . . .
I hope to live in peace,
To live in equality,
To live in harmony.

For one day . . .
I dream about a silent world,
About a state of total calm,
About a world of peace.

Just for one day . . . I wish,
Just for one day . . . I hope,
Just for one day . . . I dream.

Bethany Adler-Smith (13)
Etone College, Nuneaton

War . . . ?

War . . . What is the point of it?
War . . . What will become of it?
War . . . How can we put a stop to it?
Wars rage around the globe, from petty fights, to decade-long conflicts,
Drug dealers fighting over territory, soldiers fighting for their country
And loved ones back home.
Why? Humans weren't made to fight . . . they were made to love and to care.
So what went wrong? Why did we pick up arms and fight against our brothers?
Why? Old men who seventy years ago were sitting behind sandbags trying to think of the good times in their life,
But they always drift back to the memories of war.
Why should a soldier who was wounded in action get a £16 pension
Whereas his fellow soldier got a £100+ a week pension.
War, war, war. Why? Why? Why?

Jamie Downs (13)
Etone College, Nuneaton

Mystery?

Blood, blood, blood
It chants in the howling night
A figure as swift as air
As dark as shadows
Travels under a starry night
Crimson eyes that could pierce with one glance
Burst with hunger
Fast as lightning when it comes
You won't even realise
Teeth as white as pearls glow in the dark
The creature's eyes lock with mine
Now there is . . .
Pure darkness.

Quddoosiyyah Esmail (13)
Etone College, Nuneaton

My Life Is A Battle

I hide in the day,
I hide in the night,
I look for food,
But sadly find no one,
My life is a battle.

I'm ill in the day,
I'm ill in the night,
My health gets worse,
So I have to fight,
My life is a battle.

I cry in the day,
I cry in the night,
I comfort my sisters
Because guns cause a fight,
My life is a battle.

Mark Parlett (11)
Etone College, Nuneaton

My Pony, My Best Friend!

I love to ride my horse,
Across the fields we go,
No matter what the weather,
Come rain or wind or snow.

We canter, trot and gallop
As happy as can be.
When I'm sitting on my horse,
My life feels so carefree.

We spend our time together,
On my horse I do depend,
Not only is he special,
He's also my best friend.

Chelsea Parker (12)
Etone College, Nuneaton

Unique!

Every leaf that dances down
Every branch that curls off
Every heart that beats
Every minute, second, hour that goes by.

Every animal that is loved
Every colour that is mixed
Every cloud that moves
Every love that is given weaker or stronger.

Every star that shines
Every raindrop that falls
Every ink that hits the page
Every word that comes out of your mouth

The world matters to me
The world is unique.

Lucee Read (12)
Etone College, Nuneaton

What Matters To Me

I like the PS2
I like the PS2
I like playing all day
I like playing war games
I like the PS2
I like the PS2
I like to play with it all week
I like to play with my dad
I like the PS2
I like the PS2
I like to play car games
I like the PS2
What matters to me
I wish I had a PS3.

Lewis Humphriss (11)
Etone College, Nuneaton

What Matters To Me?

What matters to me

Is my family, they're great
And I'm just glad that they're never late

And my friends are the best
Cos they help me in tests

And my pets Twister and Blaster are fantastic
And luckily they ain't made of plastic

And my birthday I love it
In the day I love every bit

And Christmas Day with my presents
I hope that we don't eat pheasant

These are the things that matter to me
These are the things that matter mostly.

Dylan Ogilvie (12)
Etone College, Nuneaton

Sleeping

Sleeping is my favourite thing,
My bed is royal like a king,
Every night I have a dream,
Sometimes about a little stream,
My bed is very warm,
Although I can't sleep in a storm,
Sleep is what matters to me,
And it is free!

Courtney Gould (12)
Etone College, Nuneaton

One Night Is Such A Short Time

One night alone is such a short time,
With wolves howling over the horizon,
The lights began to flicker . . .

The pale blue unearthly light,
Turned into a deep red light,
As red as lava.

Thunder descended from the sky,
And those that were dead . . .
Awoken!

A man placed a crucifix in his pocket,
And gazed out of the window,
And what appeared in front of his eyes
We do imagine.

Georgie Bedford (12)
Etone College, Nuneaton

Cricket And Football

Bang goes the cricket ball,
Crack goes the cricket bat,
Ouch goes the fielder who falls,
Please could I get a new bat,
I'll just crack them all.
I love football, but the ref always calls handball,
My favourite player is Sol Campbell,
Although he moved to Newcastle.

Musa Karolia (11)
Etone College, Nuneaton

A Day At The Beach!

The sand is as hot as a radiator,
As white as fresh snow,
As grainy as sugar lumps!

Not many clouds above you,
But still you stare at their shapes,
You wait until it's moonlight,
When the sea reflects your face.

The sea moves slowly up the sand,
Biting people's toes,
It acts like a shower,
Spraying everyone with every wave.

When it's dark at night,
You lie on the damp sand,
Waving goodbye to the wonderful beach . . .

Emily Bell (11)
Etone College, Nuneaton

My Brother

My brother is so sweet
My brother is so cool
My brother is abnormal
My brother is a fool
My brother bumps his tiny head
My brother is totally well fed
My brother hits my little sister
My brother is a naughty mister
My brother is one year old
My brother is half bald
My brother fights with my mum and dad
My brother is not so bad
This boy is like no other
And this boy is my cute brother.

Rumana Sheikh (12)
Etone College, Nuneaton

Warhammer 40K!

Bang, bang! The Space Marines are down.
Smash, smash! The Tyranids come down.
The Space Marines, the finest warriors of the Imperium of Man.
The Tyranids, savage beasts that want to kill and eat everything.
Space Marines drop pods, blockout the sun like a giant black curtain.
Mycetic spores (Tyranid drop pods) block out the other two suns.
Slash, crash, bang, 'Arrrggghhh!'
The noises come from all directions.
Slash, slice!
10 million lifeless Tyranids lie on the floor.
50 million Space Marines lay breathless forever.
The Games Workshop's gone crazy.
They clear the gameboard,
Ready for the next battle,
This is Warhammer 40K!

Ryan Lucas (12)
Etone College, Nuneaton

Home

It's morning time, I leave the house,
I prepare myself for the day.
I do what I do, I do what I like,
But I always come back home.

I get picked up, I leave again,
I prepare myself for the day.
I like what I do, I do what I like,
But I always come back home.

I have a bad day, I want to come back,
I try and prepare myself for tonight,
Where I like what I like and do what I do,
I always come back home.

Lucy Price (13)
Etone College, Nuneaton

Oblivion

The evil things from other worlds
are let loose tonight,
the gates of oblivion are open
and demons run across the land . . .

The skies burn and cities fall
at Lord Dagon's delight,
the wave of death sweeps across the world
covering it in a veil of black.

Dead bodies strewn everywhere,
by the dadric hoards,
their claws tear, teeth rip,
they are the souls that cannot fly.

David Manns (12)
Etone College, Nuneaton

Missing?

What does missing mean?
Does it cause pain?
Can it ruin your life?
What does it feel like?

Missing has two different meanings.
When someone is missing from home,
When you have lost your partner.

To some people it does mean they cry over it
But some ignore the pain.

It can ruin your life but some people
Aren't that silly to end their life.

It feels like a sharp pain in your belly
And it can take a long time to get over it.

Kirstie Penn (13)
Etone College, Nuneaton

Earthquake!

Thud! Thud! earthquake
And the house fell rapidly.
People's belongings,
Flew right past
Everything fell, *thud, thud!*

Bits and pieces, collided, crashed.
Everywhere looked like war,
Again.
Finding something to hold onto,
Thud! Thud!

Seeing things, there and then.
Heartbreaking, neglected!
The sight pierced through me
Unbelievable, *thud, thud!*

Jessica Peat (14)
Etone College, Nuneaton

What Matters To Me Is My PS3

What matters to me is my PS3,
FIFA 11, Call of Duty,
Fighting games, wrestling games,
I want to be in the hall of fame.

What matters to me are my games,
I don't want games that are lame,
Dodgy games, little kiddy games,
Those games are out of the hall of fame.

What matters to me are my consoles,
My Wii, DS, PSP,
I really wish I had an Xbox 360,
But in the end I have to be me.

Zaki Bhaiyat (11)
Etone College, Nuneaton

Penguin In The Freezer

Somewhere in Grandma's freezer
Hidden in-between the
frozen peas.
there's an emperor penguin -
lost!
He's made a bed from Grandma's beef steaks
and some frozen chips.
This penguin, lost and small
has made friends with a cabbage stalk.
Like I say
an emperor penguin
what next?

Ceara Evans (11)
Etone College, Nuneaton

What Matters To Me

What matters to me is a hug when I am sad,
What matters to me is a chat when I am mad,
What matters to me is a new top for Christmas,
What matters to me is that my mate is glad.
Yet all of these things make me happy
There are more things to life than a cup of coffee,
As family is important and so are friends,
So let's start over and try it again.
What matters to me is the food that I get,
What matters to me are the friends I met.
What matters to me is the education I am getting,
What matters to me is the example I am setting.

Taylor Charnell (11)
Etone College, Nuneaton

Back In The Game

I love to play football,
Preparing for the kick, waiting for the ref's call,
Suddenly I get the ball, looking to pass,
There's no passes available, blast!
I dribble down the wing, scanning my options,
I pick a brilliant pass
My job is done,
Ninetieth minute I dart in the box,
Looking to score.
The ball hits the net and there's a massive roar,
Final score 1-0,
I love to play football.

Eliot Phillips (11)
Etone College, Nuneaton

The Poem Of Gold

I'd rather be silver than gold
I'd rather be young than old
I'd rather have hair than be bald
I'd rather be hot than cold
I'd rather behave instead of being told
I'd rather be cold than mould
I'd rather be sliced than rolled
I'd rather be rolled than bowled
I'd rather be old than gold
I'd rather be fresh than mould
I'd rather be bought than sold.
Peace dude, peace.

Michael Adams (11)
Etone College, Nuneaton

It Is All About Me!

I always smell like an attractive rose,
Mum always says I have a spectacular pose,
My smile is small but cheesy and sweet,
But sometimes I don't get a charming treat.

Irritatingly Dad bellows as I am not neat,
Galloping for the bus I am dreadfully late,
Today at school I made a superb mate.

As I stroll through the dull shop,
I sprint to get an ice pop,
This was a story about me,
Now please let me be.

Briony Harris (11)
Etone College, Nuneaton

Phoenix

The phoenix is a gentle creature,
Soaring through the air,
With gleaming feathers of fire,
A golden beak,
And the vision of a telescope,
It can see its prey from miles away,
For nothing can hide from this legendary creature.

Its life is eternal although it can be killed,
For it is reincarnated in the heart of a volcano,
To soar over the landscape again.

Thomas Costall (12)
Etone College, Nuneaton

The BMX Game!

I listen to the wind attacking my head with force.
I see the world race by on a course.
I feel my animal's tyres kiss the ground.
I attack the round surface with speed.
To find myself defy gravity's need.
Gravity's need to pull me down was just greed.
I stood tensed on my metal monster, Michael's the name,
I raced at this thing again to emerge with fame
But it was not to be and me and my monster fell with pain.
That was the end of my game.

Jack Neale (11)
Etone College, Nuneaton

Ice Skating

It costs a lot of money,
Though I find it funny,
It's glamorous and graceful . . .
Playful and painful,
It's skilful and can be willful,
It brings the skills and skaters out,
It makes me feel happy
And no longer a baby in a nappy.
It's unique and makes me go eeek!
And that is what matters to me.

Felicity Dodson (12)
Etone College, Nuneaton

Bamford The Rabbit

Bamford the rabbit
Has a wonderful habit
Of hopping around the garden
When the grass is starting to harden
From his twitchy nose
To his little toes
With his twinkly eyes
He's such a surprise
He's black and white
When he's in the spotlight.

Luke Perrohn (12)
Etone College, Nuneaton

Music

The guitar is strumming like a plucking string.
The man is singing like a bird tweeting.
The music is dancing like a ballerina.
The trumpet is tooting like a horn on a car.
The drums are banging like a gun firing.
The cymbals crash like a wave crashing.

Do you like music?
I like music very much!

Kieran Folan (11)
Etone College, Nuneaton

Love

Love is more than just a thing,
It means much more than anything,
Love lasts forever just like it should,
Love is a commitment stronger than wood,
Love comes from the heart not from the heels,
Love is like perfection,
Love never goes away like your reflection.

Caitlin Watson (12)
Etone College, Nuneaton

My Friends

My friends are always helping me,
Whenever I'm feeling down,
My friends are always cheering me up,
Whenever I've got a frown,
My friends always walk with me,
Whenever we're walking through town,
My friends always hang with me,
Wherever we're hanging around.

Joe Smith (11)
Etone College, Nuneaton

Are You Mean?

Hurting the world is mean,
It drives people crazy.
Wasting injures the world
And makes us get curled fists.
As we're so angry,
As people are so lazy,
To save the world from pollution.
So remember when you waste what you're doing to the world.

Aliyah Patel (11)
Etone College, Nuneaton

Cricket

Waiting for the ball to come to me, *smack,*
I hit the ball.
Running back and forth as the opposing team try to get the ball back to the stumps.
The ball is about to hit the stumps, but I just make it in.
The crowd goes wild with cheers and screams.
I like cricket, it's my favourite thing.

Fraser Powell (11)
Etone College, Nuneaton

I Think . . .

I think I can fly
Very, very high
You hit a wall again and again
You stop to deal with the pain
You kill using a flame
You give *me* the blame.

Cory Richardson (14)
Etone College, Nuneaton

What Matters

What matters to me is my family and friends
Lots of things matter to me
My family and friends are always there for me
They look after you
They buy you stuff
My family and friends are never rough
My friends are so tough
Sometimes that's just enough.

Ieuan Llewellyn (13)
Etone College, Nuneaton

The Beach

I stepped onto the white sand with the sun beaming on me
like fire hitting petrol.
I ran towards the sea and slowly stepped in,
the sea was bright blue and the waves were as white as chalk,
palm trees were swaying side to side like cars' window wipers,
the waves were crashing against the moss-covered rocks,
as the seaweed swayed against the sea.

Kirsty Folan (13)
Etone College, Nuneaton

Friends

F riends are the kind of people who are always there.
R espect each other because we care.
I f ever in doubt, they will always sort it out.
E very day we would giggle and shout.
N o days go by that we forget each other.
D ays and days we are together.
S o my mates and me will stay friends forever.

Grace Greenaway (12)
Etone College, Nuneaton

This Is What Matters To Me

The wafting smell of my burnt toast as I took a hard munch.
The sound of my feet going crunch.
The amazing chocolate fountain is playing games with my mind.
Rushing to school to get there on time.
Hanging out with my chatting friends who are bubbly.
My cute kitten who is so lovely.
This is what matters to me!

Sophia Evans (11)
Etone College, Nuneaton

Bombs

Bombs are loud and have a big explosion.
They destroy things and make people cry when some people die.
Bombs are used for wars
And they cause people to die.
Bombs make loud noises when they hit the floor
And they have big explosions.
They blow away the dirt.

Callum Cheshire (13)
Etone College, Nuneaton

What Matters To Me

What matters to me is my family
My rugby, my friends and my TV.
The place that I learn in is what matters to me.
What matters to me is my PSP,
Along with my friends and my family
And that's what matters to me.

Jack Bannister (11)
Etone College, Nuneaton

Star

The sun has gone to sleep,
a blanket drawn across the sky,
a dark blanket with rips and holes,
as the sun falls asleep,
the glow seeps through the holes,
her new name is Star.

Rosie Parsons (13)
Etone College, Nuneaton

The War

The guns were rapidly firing.
The tracks of tanks everywhere.
The people were shouting like a lion in pain.
The explosions of grenades everywhere.
The flame-throwers look like mini suns from the air.
The planes like swarms of fleas in the air.

Jacob Lloyd (11)
Etone College, Nuneaton

Feelings And Colours

I am red today, angry as a roaring fire,
I am yellow today, bubbly as a bubble bath,
I am grey today, not too hot, not too cold, like a raincloud,
I am blue today, sad as a lost duckling,
I am pink today, happy as Larry,
I am orange today, bright as sunshine.

Jessica Bate (13)
Etone College, Nuneaton

The Greatest Gift?

Life?
When you first peer into the world,
Through newborn eyes,
When everything is so innocent,
Before it all dies.

The task of growing up,
Spreading wings like a dove,
Filling our lives with joy,
Things like indescribable love,

Friends?
The loyal companions,
Always at your side,
Embracing your heart,
Till the day they lied,

They feel as close as family,
Warm like the sun,
Until they turn around,
And high tail and run,

Family?
Mother and father,
Through the good and bad,
Keeping you close,
When you feel sad,

Bringing you up as a kid,
Teaching you right from wrong,
A dreary pattern,
Sung in song,

Music?
The frantic drumbeats,
In time to your heart,
Counting down,
Until the start,

Guitar riffs and solos,
Low hum of the bass,
A slow tune of silence,
Echoing into space,

Money?
A single piece of paper,
Earning you power and greed,
One piece and you're hooked,
For it is the green on which you must feed,

A small thin coin,
We throw it all away,
Small copper and metal,
Don't we have a say,

Health?
Keeping the illness at bay,
With a few simple pills,
But it doesn't always work,
Sometimes it kills,

Make way for me,
I don't feel well,
Please help cure me,
It hurt when I fell,

Education?
The peaceful drone,
Of books galore,
Learning forever,
The rich and the poor,

Writing essays,
And checking over work,
Re-reading stories,
Will send you all berserk,

Nature?
The soft petals of a rose,
And the strong bark of the trees,
Stand no chance,
Against the hurricane breeze,

Daisies and dandelions,
Covered in bugs,
Cocaine and marijuana,
Are all senseless drugs,

Memory?

A happy thought,
To relive the past,
When a close family member,
Took their breath as last,

Do you remember,
All those good times,
A sense of déjà vu,
Small little insignificant signs,

Love?
Your first kiss,
A frantic heartbeat,
You told me you loved me,
All lies of deceit,

Is that all it takes?
My innocence shattered,
I can't take it anymore,
My heart is battered,

All is close to heart,
Impossible to erase,
The good and the bad,
It seems to be the case,
They come in twos,
The dark and the light,
If you do not understand,
You were born without sight.

Jennifer Walton (15)
St James' CE Secondary School, Farnworth

Home Sweet Home - Haiku

My home is massive,
It's clean and very tidy,
My house is super!

Ryan Kitchen (11)
St James' CE Secondary School, Farnworth

Simply Sweet Home

My house is made of walls and beams,
My home is not where my doorbell rings
My home is built with love and dreams,
My home is not where I keep my things.

My home is not where my memories lie,
Where I grew up makes me wonder why

It surrounds me with warmth like a comforting throne,
My life makes more sense, the world seems true
Being wrapped in your arms is where I call my home,
I love my home, I really do . . .

It's where your secrets are kept,
Yet home is where you've wept

Where does the world start?
At my door . . .
Where does the world end?
At my door . . .

So . . . this is the kind of home I live in
This provides love, care and being there for each other

People say, 'There's no place like home.'

Roshni Dhodakia (12)
St James' CE Secondary School, Farnworth

My House - Haiku

Warm, comfy and safe
A place where you can relax
Home. It's snuggly.

Ellie Cook (11)
St James' CE Secondary School, Farnworth

More Than One Home - Haikus

Home wonderful home
My warm, cosy home
It's the place I love the most
Mum, Dad, Alice, me

One less cosy home
Outdoors isn't best
It's the only place for some
Poor and unlucky

Carrying a shell
A snail's life is hard
Slither, slime, crushed all the time
Their home on their back

A dog's home
Some kind, some horrid
They run all day, bark at night
Some neighbours complain

Rich and famous
Very big mansion
Swimming pools, butlers, cocktails
Really love my life

On the move again
I move every day
My caravan comes and goes
On the move again.

Molly Costello (11)
St James' CE Secondary School, Farnworth

Home Forever

My house is fun
and I have a big car.
I love my mum
and it isn't very far
and we could never leave
anyone or anything
and we are always good
I'm friends with Neve
and we all can't sing.

Lauren Tonge (12)
St James' CE Secondary School, Farnworth

My Home - Haiku

I feel safe and warm
And I feel happy at home
I feel warm at home.

Luke Williams (11)
St James' CE Secondary School, Farnworth

Autumn Leaves

Autumn leaves
Falling to the ground
I watch a leaf settle down
On a bed of brown.

Alannah Pierce-Jackson (11)
St James' CE Secondary School, Farnworth

Ode To Home

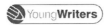

I have a home,
Like everyone has,
But my home,
Is my home,
It's not big,
It's not small,
It's not perfect,
It's not rubbish,
It's not dirty,
It's not clean,
It's not pretty,
It's not ugly,
It's not cold,
It's not hot,
It's not old,
It's not new,
It's not colourful,
It's not dull,
But it is expensive,
My home is my home.

Idnan Ahmed (12)
St James' CE Secondary School, Farnworth

My House - Haiku

My house is so warm
And so comfy it also
Keeps me protected.

Harvey Townsend (11)
St James' CE Secondary School, Farnworth

Ode To Home

Slowly slither
In the dirt
Now I'm hurt
If you help
You will hear
A giant yelp!
And a scream of fear!

Now I'm out
I'm on the street
It's hard to find
Something to eat
I wouldn't mind
A piece of meat
As long as it
Doesn't taste like feet.

Winter's here
And it's cold
Now I'm withered
And very old
If I die
You won't know
Someone's dropped
A very nice bow.

Aqil Chachia (12)
St James' CE Secondary School, Farnworth

My Haiku

Lying on the ground
Dreaming of his fantasy
But wakes up to Hell.

Arif Bham (11)
St James' CE Secondary School, Farnworth

Ode To Home

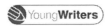

Home sweet home
Nowhere else is better
If I could go anywhere
I'd wanna go home,
Home sweet home.

I'd rather go home
Than play with a bone
I just wanna go home.
Home sweet home.

I'd rather go home
Than get a new phone
I just wanna go home.
Home sweet home.

I'd rather go home
Than fly about in a dome,
I just wanna go home.
Home sweet home.

George Miller (12)
St James' CE Secondary School, Farnworth

Home Sweet Home

My home is the safest place to be
My dog greets me at the door
As I lock the door with my key
I need to be careful on this slippery floor
I dump my bags and go into the back room
Switch on the telly and have a cup of tea
My mum's in the kitchen tidying up
My dad walks in with a bang and a boom
How noisy can he be?
I am so glad this home is mine
I am so happy and filled with pride.

Amelia Thomas (12)
St James' CE Secondary School, Farnworth

Featured Poets:
DEAD POETS
AKA Mark Grist & MC Mixy

Mark Grist and MC Mixy joined forces to become the 'Dead Poets' in 2008.

Since then Mark and Mixy have been challenging the preconceptions of poetry and hip hop across the country. As 'Dead Poets', they have performed in venues ranging from nightclubs to secondary schools; from festivals to formal dinners. They've appeared on Radio 6 Live with Steve Merchant, they've been on a national tour with Phrased and Confused and debuted their show at the 2010 Edinburgh Fringe, which was a huge success.

Both Mark and Mixy work on solo projects as well as working together as the 'Dead Poets'. Both have been Peterborough's Poet Laureate, with Mixy holding the title for 2010.

The 'Dead Poets' are available for workshops in your school as well as other events. Visit www.deadpoetry.co.uk for further information and to contact the guys!

Read on to pick up some fab writing tips!

Your WORKSHOPS

In these workshops we are going to look at writing styles and examine some literary techniques that the 'dead poets' use. Grab a pen, and let's go!

Rhythm Workshop

Rhythm in writing is like the beat in music. Rhythm is when certain words are produced more forcefully than others, and may be held for longer duration. The repetition of a pattern is what produces a 'rhythmic effect'. The word rhythm comes from the Greek meaning of 'measured motion'.

Count the number of syllables in your name. Then count the number of syllables in the following line, which you write in your notepad: 'My horse, my horse, will not eat grass'.

Now, highlight the longer sounding syllables and then the shorter sounding syllables in a different colour.

Di dum, di dum, di dum, di dum is a good way of summing this up.

You should then try to write your own lines that match this rhythm. You have one minute to see how many you can write!

Examples include:
'My cheese smells bad because it's hot'
and
'I do not like to write in rhyme'.

For your poem, why don't you try to play with the rhythm? Use only longer beats or shorter beats? Create your own beat and write your lines to this?

Did you know ... ?

Did you know that paper was invented in China around 105AD by Ts'ai Lun. The first English paper mill didn't open until 1590 and was in Dartford.

Rhyme Workshop

Start off with the phrase 'I'd rather be silver than gold' in your notepad. and see if you can come up with lines that rhyme with it -
'I'd rather have hair than be bald'
'I'd rather be young than be old'
'I'd rather be hot than cold'
'I'd rather be bought than sold'

Also, pick one of these words and see how many rhymes you can find:

Rose

Wall

Warm

Danger

What kinds of rhymes did you come up with? Are there differences in rhymes? Do some words rhyme more cleanly than others? Which do you prefer and why?

Lists Workshop

Game - you (and you can ask your friends or family too) to write as many reasons as possible for the following topics:

Annoying things about siblings

The worst pets ever

The most disgusting ingredients for a soup you can think of

Why not try writing a poem with the same first 2, 3 or 4 words?

I am ...

Or

I love it when ...

Eg:

I am a brother

I am a listener

I am a collector of secrets

I am a messer of bedrooms.

Onomatopoeia Workshop

Divide a sheet of A4 paper into 8 squares.

You then have thirty seconds to draw/write what could make the following sounds:

Splash	Ping
Drip	Bang
Rip	Croak
Crack	Splash

Now try writing your own ideas of onomatopoeia. Why might a writer include onomatopoeia in their writing?

Repetition Workshop

Come up with a list of words/ phrases, aim for at least 5. You now must include one of these words in your piece at least 6 times. You aren't allowed to place these words/ phrases at the beginning of any of the lines.

Suggested words/phrases:

Why

Freedom

Laughing

That was the best day ever

I can't find the door

I'm in trouble again

The best

Workshop POETRY 101

Below is a poem written especially for Poetry Matters, by MC Mixy.
Why not try and write some more poems of your own?

What is Matter?

© MC Mixy

What matters to me may not be the same things that matter to you
You may not agree with my opinion mentality or attitude
The order in which I line up my priorities to move
Choose to include my view and do what I do due to my mood
And state of mind
I make the time to place the lines on stacks of paper and binds
Concentrate on my artwork hard I can't just pass and scrape behind
Always keep close mates of mine that make things right
And even those who can't … just cos I love the way they can try
What matters to me is doing things the right way
It's tough this game of life we play what we think might stray from what others might say
In this world of individuality we all wanna bring originality
Live life and drift through casually but the vicious reality is
Creativity is unique
Opinions will always differ but if you figure you know the truth, speak
So many things matter to me depending on how tragically deep you wanna go
I know I need to defy gravity on this balance beam
As I laugh and breathe draft and read map the scene practise piece smash the beat and graphic release
Visual and vocal it's a standard procedure
Have to believe and don't bite the hand when it feeds ya

If you wanna be a leader you need to stay out of the pen where the sheep are
The things that matter to me are
My art and my friends
That will stay from the start to the end
People will do things you find hard to amend
Expect the attacks and prepare you gotta be smart to defend
I put my whole heart in the blend the mass is halved yet again
I'm marked by my pen a big fish fighting sharks of men
In a small pond
Dodging harpoons and nets hooks and predators tryna dismember ya
I won't let them I won't get disheartened I can fend for myself
As long as I'm doing what's important
I'm my mind where I'm supported is a just cause to be supporting
In these appalling hard times I often find myself falling when
Only two aspects of my life keep me sane and allow me to stand tall again
Out of all of them two is a small number
It's a reminder I remind ya to hold necessity and let luxury fall under
Try to avoid letting depression seep through
Take the lesson we actually need a lot less than we think we do
So what matters to you?
They may be similar to things that matter to me
I'm actually lacking the need of things I feel would help me to succeed
Though I like to keep it simple, I wanna love, I wanna breed
I'm one of many individuals in this world where importance fluctuates and varies
Things that matter will come and go
But the ones that stay for long enough must be worth keeping close
If you're not sure now don't watch it you'll know when you need to know
Me, I think I know now … yet I feel and fear I don't.

Turn overleaf for a poem by Mark Grist and some fantastic hints and tips!

Workshop POETRY 101

What Tie Should I Wear Today?

© Mark Grist

I wish I had a tie that was suave and silk and slick,
One with flair, that's debonair and would enchant with just one flick,
Yeah, I'd like that … a tie that's hypnotizing,
I'd be very restrained and avoid womanising,
But all the lady teachers would still say 'Mr Grist your tie's so charming!'
As I cruise into their classrooms with it striking and disarming.
At parents' evenings my tie's charm would suffice,
In getting mums to whisper as they leave 'Your English teacher seems nice!'

Or maybe an evil-looking tie - one that's the business,
Where students will go 'Watch out! Mr Grist is
on the prowl with that evil tie.'
The one that cornered Josh and then ripped out his eye.
Yeah no one ever whispers, no one ever sniggers,
Or my tie would rear up and you'd wet your knickers.
Maybe one girl just hasn't heard the warning,
Cos she overslept and turned up late to school that morning,
And so I'd catch her in my lesson yawning … oh dear.
I'd try to calm it down, but this tie's got bad ideas.
It'd size the girl up and then just as she fears,
Dive in like a serpent snapping at her ears.
There'd be a scream, some blood and lots and lots of tears,
And she wouldn't be able to yawn again for years.

Or maybe … a tie that everyone agrees is mighty fine
And people travel from miles around to gawp at the design
I'd like that … a tie that pushes the boundaries of tieware right up to the limit
It'd make emos wipe their tears away while chavs say 'It's wicked innit?'
and footy lads would stop me with 'I'd wear that if I ever won the cup.'
And I'd walk through Peterborough to slapped backs, high fives, thumbs up
While monosyllabic teenagers would just stand there going 'Yup.'

I don't know. I'd never be sure which of the three to try
As any decision between them would always end a tie.

Tips and Advice for PERFORMING Your Poem

So you've written your poem, now how about performing it. Whether you read your poem for the first time in front of your class, school or strangers at an open mic event or poetry slam, these tips will help you make the best of your performance.

Breathe and try to relax.

Every poet that reads in front of people for the first time feels a bit nervous, when you're there you are in charge and nothing serious can go wrong.

People at poetry slams or readings are there to support the poets. They really are!

If you can learn your poem off by heart that is brilliant, however having a piece of paper or notebook with your work in is fine, though try not to hide behind these.

It's better to get some eye contact with the audience. If you're nervous find a friendly face to focus on.

Try to read slowly and clearly and enjoy your time in the spotlight.

Don't rush up to the microphone, make sure it's at the right height for you and if you need it adjusted ask one of the team around you.

Before you start, stand up as straight as you can and get your body as comfortable as you can and remember to hold your head up.

The microphone can only amplify what what's spoken into it; if you're very loud you might end up deafening people and if you only whisper or stand too far away you won't be heard.

When you say something before your poem, whether that's hello or just the title of your poem, try and have a listen to how loud you sound. If you're too quiet move closer to the microphone, if you're too loud move back a bit.

Remember to breathe! Don't try to say your poem so quickly you can't find time to catch your breath.

And finally, **enjoy!**

Poetry FACTS

Here are a selection of fascinating poetry facts!

No word in the English language rhymes with 'MONTH'.

William Shakespeare was born on 23rd April 1564 and died on 23rd April 1616.

The haiku is one of the shortest forms of poetic writing. Originating in Japan, a haiku poem is only seventeen syllables, typically broken down into three lines of five, seven and five syllables respectively.

The motto of the Globe Theatre was 'totus mundus agit histrionem' (the whole world is a playhouse).

The Children's Laureate award was an idea by Ted Hughes and Michael Morpurgo.

The 25th January each year is Burns' Night, an occasion in honour of Scotland's national poet Robert Burns.

Spike Milligan's 'On the Ning Nang Nong' was voted the UK's favourite comic poem in 1998.

Did you know *onomatopoeia* means the word you use sounds like the word you are describing – like the rain *pitter-patters* or the snow *crunches* under my foot.

'Go' is the shortest complete sentence in the English language.

Did you know rhymes were used in olden days to help people remember the news? Ring-o'-roses is about the Plague!

The Nursery Rhyme 'Old King Cole' is based on a real king and a real historical event. King Cole is supposed to have been an actual monarch of Britain who ruled around 200 A.D.

Edward Lear popularised the limerick with his poem 'The Owl and the Pussy-Cat'.

Lewis Carroll's poem 'The Jabberwocky' is written in nonsense style.

POEM – noun

1. a composition in verse, esp. one that is characterized by a highly developed artistic form and by the use of heightened language and rhythm to express an intensely imaginative interpretation of the subject.

Poetry TIPS
We have compiled some helpful tips for you budding poets...

In order to write poetry, read lots of poetry!

Keep a notebook with you at all times so you can write whenever (and wherever) inspiration strikes.

Every line of a poem should be important to the poem and interesting to read. A poem with only 3 great lines should be 3 lines long.

Use an online rhyming dictionary to improve your vocabulary.

Use free workshops and help sheets to learn new poetry styles.

Experiment with visual patterns - does your written poetry create a good pattern on the page?

Try to create pictures in the reader's mind - aim to fire the imagination.

Develop your voice. Become comfortable with how you write.

Listen to criticism, and try to learn from it, but don't live or die by it.

Say what you want to say, let the reader decide what it means.

Notice what makes other's poetry memorable. Capture it, mix it up and make it your own. (Don't copy other's work word for word!)

Go wild. Be funny. Be serious. Be whatever you want!

Grab hold of something you feel - anything you feel - and write it.

The more you write, the more you develop. Write poetry often.

Use your imagination, your own way of seeing.

Feel free to write a bad poem, it will develop your 'voice'.

Did you know ...?

'The Epic of Gilgamesh' was written thousands of years ago in Mesopotamia and is the oldest poem on record.

An Ode To Home

A home is a home no matter how big
A home is a home even to pigs
A home is something to look forward to when you're out
A home is something that keeps you sheltered
In the rain even if you're in pain,
A home is a relaxing place
So make the most of your home.

A home puts a smile on your face
A home makes you feel happy,
A home is a place where you could play your PS3
A home is a place where you can kick back,
Relax, watch some telly and say home sweet home.

There's nothing better than a home,
A home's special, so treasure it like gold,
A home has a very comfy bed,
I know I love my home,
So the question is do you?

Muhammad Adia (12)
St James' CE Secondary School, Farnworth

Home Again - Haikus

There are loads of homes around the world.

It is snuggly
I like my beautiful home
It's clean and tidy

I have lots of gold
My home is made of money
I have a monkey

I live with the rats
My clothes are falling apart
I feel so exposed.

Shivam Patel (11)
St James' CE Secondary School, Farnworth

Snails

Slimy and slippery,
Snails are such fun,
Greasy and grimy,
They can't even run!

On their back is a shell,
It's really their home,
It's ever so small,
But it goes where they roam.

The shell is so hard,
It's got a design!
It'll send me a yard,
But I'll be fine.

Shiny and slippery,
Snails are such fun,
They eat and they eat,
They must weigh a ton!

Yameen Mallu (12)
St James' CE Secondary School, Farnworth

About A Home!

A home is somewhere to keep warm,
Somewhere you can eat,
This is a place you don't have to be alarmed,
For example to eat meat,
This is somewhere you can sleep,
You can also relax,
It's very, very sweet,
In this place you can weep,
And relax like my dog, Max,
A home is somewhere you're mostly with your family,
For me, my mum and my dad, Pete.

Burnden Lee Horrocks (12)
St James' CE Secondary School, Farnworth

My Home

My home
is a relaxing
place to be.
It's a nice place
to live.
My home's an awesome place
to have some tea.
We probably even own a sieve!
My home, I love
it to bits
because it's the place
I own.
The best room in the house
is the kitchen
for the biscuits.
You can never get me
off the phone.

Samantha Young (12)
St James' CE Secondary School, Farnworth

Home!

My house is exciting,
My best room is the living room.
I go on my PS3 on fighting.
My bedroom is full of gloom.
I play out on my lawn.
My house is comfy.
I'm sometimes happy.
I sometimes moan.
My dog is called Humphrey,
I have a goldfish,
Called Slappy.

James Lord (12)
St James' CE Secondary School, Farnworth

Home Sweet Home - Haikus

I live in a shop
It has bright gold plated floors
And it has a door.

My bedroom is huge
With cream and white wallpaper
With a king-size bed.

I sit in my room
Staring out my big window
There are birds tweeting

I don't have a house
I am freezing and hungry
Give me some money.

I am very rich
Servants that clean up get gifts
I own a mansion.

Binisha Harivadan Vekaria (12)
St James' CE Secondary School, Farnworth

Haiku

My home is so great
My house is sweet and supreme
My house is special.

Haroon Parvez (11)
St James' CE Secondary School, Farnworth

Sweet Home - Haikus

Beloved home
Beloved warm home
Very comfortable for me
A lovely, safe place.

Paradise home
I was excited
I had everything at home
And a lovely place.

My cat
Beloved grey cat
Curls up softly in my lap
Furry loyal friend.

Hasan Patel (11)
St James' CE Secondary School, Farnworth

So Beautiful!

You are so beautiful, so very beautiful,
Your soul has risen from the almighty heavens,
The homely feeling, ahh blissful,
You breeze the thought of another school morning
While the world awakens

The heart and desire to let me sleep in peace,
The aroma of the sumptuous food in the kitchen,
While I watch the exciting horse race,
The sizzle, sizzle, sizzle of the delectable chicken

Our wonderful home,
It is so beautiful,
Makes me cuddlesome!

Dhillon Lad (12)
St James' CE Secondary School, Farnworth

No Place Like Home - Haikus

There's no place like home
Lions stretching out their legs!
Free at last from you!

All that remains of
My home sweet home is the smell,
Of sweet-smelling grass!

Resting at my home,
Heaven came to me at last!
Gold, silver, bronze coins!

Home is beautiful!
Home is comfy and cosy,
Home sweet lovely home!

Home you are smelly!
You stink of black smelly socks!
I wish I could move!

Ammarah Rawat (12)
St James' CE Secondary School, Farnworth

Ode To Home!

My favourite room is my bedroom,
Always keeping calm on my bed,
When doing homework for Mr Hulme.
Keeping all the information in my head,
Playing basketball in my backyard,
Always keeping fit and healthy,
Stay indoors and finish homework.
My dog remains keeping guard,
Grow older and become wealthy,
Before my dad gets home from work!

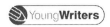

Rudra Dave (12)
St James' CE Secondary School, Farnworth

The Home Of A Cheetah - Haikus

The cheetah stretches.
Silently she stalks her prey.
The antelope eats.

Grazing on the grass,
He does not sense the danger.
He feels calm and safe.

The cheetah strikes out.
The antelope has no chance.
She takes home her prey.

She carries him off,
Her jaw is tight as he kicks.
The cheetah is home.

Vultures are waiting.
They circle the cheetah's home.
They want to eat too.

Callum Foster (11)
St James' CE Secondary School, Farnworth

Joys Of Caravans - Haiku

Homes are on the move,
Clean, comfort and filled with joy
Special joys of life.

Akash Gujjar (11)
St James' CE Secondary School, Farnworth

An Ode To Home

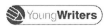

My home is comfy,
It's never too lumpy,
It's a place to stay,
When I've come back from away
It's nice to have your own set of keys,
A place to stay away from the bees
With a TV and a sofa,
And even your own chauffeur.

It comes with a kitchen and windows,
And an occasional box of Lindors.
It's never too far or never too close,
And a mailbox to get your post.
My bedroom is up the stairs
And a room my mum and dad share.
My home is a special place,
The people inside are the base.

Zain Ahmed (12)
St James' CE Secondary School, Farnworth

I Like . . .

I live in a house, it's a lovely little house
and I live with my family, Mum, Dad and sister Holly.
I love our little house,
it's never quiet like a mouse.
I have a friend from next door called Molly
we always have lots of fun
and do lots of stuff together.
I don't care about what others think, my house is by far the best,
so no crimes round my house, no guns,
I know my family will love me forever.
For the best family we would win that test.

Libby Cowburn (12)
St James' CE Secondary School, Farnworth

Haikus

My house's tall and wide
My house is made out of bricks
My house is my house.

My house is so big
My house is in Westhoughton
My house has three floors.

My room is a mess
It has posters and drawings
It is warm and snug.

My garden is great
It has flowers, garden gnomes
It has nice wildlife.

Rebekah Coghlin (11)
St James' CE Secondary School, Farnworth

Home

My house is a star
It's as sweet as candy
It's as helpful as a car
Sometimes I need friends like Andy.

I am always happy
When I'm, having fun
However when I have to change my cousin's nappy
I feel like shooting someone with the gun.

My family is sweet
That's why I love my family a lot,
Every day we wake up and hear the birds tweet
If the food is hot.

That's when we shout.
That's why it's a lovely home.

Rutendo Dhandinda (12)
St James' CE Secondary School, Farnworth

An Ode To Home

My Xbox, my TV, my room, my bed?
Without you home, I'd be dead.
Without you home, I'd be shedding tears,
Without you home, I'd have the right to fear.

Without you home, where would I sleep?
Without you home, where could I pack my Jeep?
Without you home, where could I play my Xbox?
Without you home, where would I put my socks?

Without you home, where can I put my clothes?
Without you home, where can I wash my nose?
Without you home, where would I live?
And where would I put my sieve?

Ismail Adia (13)
St James' CE Secondary School, Farnworth

Ode To Home

My home is quite a sight
The wonder and delight
You stand up tall
Conscious of all
You keep me nice and warm
Especially when there is a storm
And as you stand in the winter breeze
If I was there I'd probably freeze.

If I'm in you
Other people can see you
When I am down
You take away my frown
Home, you're the best
Better than the rest.

Niall Airey (12)
St James' CE Secondary School, Farnworth

An Ode To Home

Home, what is home?
Home is great
Home is a treat
Home is as extremely delightful as the moon
Unless you live in the state of a baboon.

A place where you can sleep
A place where you can eat
A place where you can share
A place where you can be fair.

Your home is the place where you are free
And can enjoy your life joyfully
Just open the door and you will see
That you can always stay free.

This is what a home is!

Faisal Kaduji (12)
St James' CE Secondary School, Farnworth

Animal Hunting Poem

I'm a wild beast,
Unknown to all around,
I'm searching for a feast,
Worthy of a king, rulers of the ground.
Am I able to complete
My task of taking life?
I am hunting now,
Would it be possible to cheat?
My internal strife,
I've no need for my master to show me how,
How to accomplish my mission,
I must gorge myself till I'm ill,
I have pounced and given away my position,
That's it, the deed is done, I've made the kill.

Nicole Tyler (13)
St James' CE Secondary School, Farnworth

Home Sweet Home - Haikus

Please will you come in,
Shall I turn the heating up?
Would you like a drink?

Thank you very much,
This chair's so comfortable,
This room is awesome.

Would you like some food?
And shall I invite our mates?
Yes, that would be great.

I had a great time,
Now it's time for me to go,
See you later, bye.

Joshua John Thompson (11)
St James' CE Secondary School, Farnworth

My Dream Home

Lush leather chairs await
Home, sweet home which I adore
How lovely it is.

Luscious home
Warm, toasty and quiet, how peaceful
Sitting in Heaven.

My favourite room
My bed warm and snuggly
Dreaming peacefully.

Hot, toasty, warm bath
I love sitting in the tub
It is very, very nice!

Tejal Rana (11)
St James' CE Secondary School, Farnworth

The Devil's Playhouse - Haikus

I searched the whole room,
Where the hot flames scorched at me,
Then the Devil came.

I was so frightened,
I didn't know what to do,
So I ran quickly.

I wished I was home,
But I was at the Devil's,
How did I get there?

But that moment
I ended up at my home,
What just happened then?

Amir Kala (11)
St James' CE Secondary School, Farnworth

Homely Home - Haikus

It is dark at night
Dogs are howling as you sleep
Suddenly hands show

It is amazing
It's just like a cinema
Everything's perfect

I'm in all alone
I hear creaking, lights flicker
You try to escape

Not once should I sit
For there is so much to do
When seated relaxed.

Chris Galley (11)
St James' CE Secondary School, Farnworth

The Castle - Haikus

The empty castle,
My voice echoes around me,
The castle, my home!

I am so lonely,
I have no one to see there,
The castle, my home.

There is a graveyard,
My family are in there,
The castle, my home.

I hear their voices,
They echo all around me,
The castle, my home!

Holly Ghoorun (11)
St James' CE Secondary School, Farnworth

Home Sweet Home - Haikus

I stared at my bed,
My comfy, relaxing bed.
Then I fell asleep!

I stared at the room,
The nice, warm fire burning
My face has gone red!

The kitchen awaits,
Brew time, the kettle is on.
The sweet taste of tea.

My nice, clean bathroom!
As I step in the shower,
I feel home sweet home.

Nisha Patel (11)
St James' CE Secondary School, Farnworth

Home Sweet Home - Haikus

As I cried I stared
And wondered where are the stars
The stars are up high.

In my house I die
The neighbours cry, even I
Don't know what to do.

After a long, hard
Day I come to my house and
Wish my fears away.

In my house I go
Through everything such as these:
Tears, laughter, joy, fun!

Jessica Furness (11)
St James' CE Secondary School, Farnworth

My House!

Mars Avenue is the name of my street
I know it sounds lame and weird
But it's really cool and really sweet
And I sometimes say it's luck
My house is full of laughter and pride
It's been standing for over 80 years
And hasn't ever collapsed.
When my mum and dad bought it they cried
And said, 'Whoo, home!' and had a few beers
But will I find the true meaning of a house?
Maybe one day perhaps.

Neve Rosevere (12)
St James' CE Secondary School, Farnworth

Dream Home - Haikus

I looked at my house
It was massive and cosy
I wanted to hug it.

I stared at my bed
Filled with money and hard gold
Shining brightly now.

I stared at the room
Gold carpet and smooth silk bed
I have a great house.

I stared at the wall
Smooth and ruby red paper
A beautiful wall.

Usamah Khan (11)
St James' CE Secondary School, Farnworth

My House

Home is warm
It's my own space
Where me and my friends swarm
My own place

Home is full of love
Full of peace
Full of stuff

Home is like a beautiful flying dove
Where my brother is a beast
My home has had enough!

Nadiya Patel (12)
St James' CE Secondary School, Farnworth

Shell Of The Snail

The snail lives inside a shell, light brown,
To us it is junk - a bit of litter,
But to the snail paradise, joy and a crown,
And without it? Phew! life would be bitter . . .

A home should be safe, cosy and snug.
The snail gets all that from that tiny shell;
Everyone has a home. But how? Just how?

Home for the snail is different from any other bug.
With a shell, rain, snow, frost is sure to repel,
Sure enough right now snails are slithering and in shells now . . .

Rebecca Tracey (13)
St James' CE Secondary School, Farnworth

Home

Home is a place that is always there
A home that desires our love
Home is place where we all care
A place we all know of

Home is where the heart lies
It's where we all belong
Home is a light that will always shine

Home is a place that puts a gleam in your eye
It's where our feelings are kept strong
I'm proud my home is mine.

Aimée Parmar (12)
St James' CE Secondary School, Farnworth

Engine

I am an engine that lives in a car.
I am the thing that helps win the race.
I do this, I travel what seems very far.
I get very hot because I don't have much space.

The flag comes down, we're off to a good start.
After three laps my tyres are getting worn.
Into the pits I go for a check.

Back in the race now, I'm faster with new parts.
'Get out of the way!' I sound my horn.
Screech! Crash! Bang! I'm in a wreck.

Robert Leyland (12)
St James' CE Secondary School, Farnworth

Ode To Home

Let me tell you about my home
The safest place you will know
Wherever I wander, wherever I roam
Back to my home I will always go.

It's calm and warm, a place for me
Filled with love and dignity
The homely feeling warms my heart
Because this is my place to be.
My family is filled with generosity
Which I miss when we're apart.

Jessica Yates (12)
St James' CE Secondary School, Farnworth

My Home

My home is the place to be
Perhaps not for you,
But it is for me
And all my friends and family too.

My home is filled with laughter and fun,
My mum, my dad, my sister and me
Inside you will also find my dog, Tommy.
We're in the garden when we see the sun.
If you were to come and see
I'm sure you'd love my home as much as me.

Jamie Whittle (12)
St James' CE Secondary School, Farnworth

My Home

My house is bright but small
We have lots of cats running wild
We have a soft carpet if we fall
But the kitchen and bathroom are tiled

My room has lots of books
My sister's room has lots of bags
My mum and dad's room has a bed with pillows
The kitchen has lots of cooks
The cars on the drive are cleaned with rags
And the garden is surrounded by weeping willows.

Rebecca Walker (12)
St James' CE Secondary School, Farnworth

Home!

My home is a safe place,
It shows me all that's great,
The happiness shows on my face,
Though some others are filled with hate.

My home makes me feel warm inside,
As I watch the flashing pictures go by,
I'm glad to say this house is mine,
And I say it with lots of pride,
It's so overwhelming it makes me cry,
I'm excited when I see it every time!

Rebecca Rose Preston (12)
St James' CE Secondary School, Farnworth

Home Sweet Home

My home is sweet
All nice and calm
Outside in the morning little birds tweet
Just two miles away there is a very clean farm.

Everyone is loving and caring
I feel very safe and proud
My room is very neat and cool
I have a pet cat which is always staring
Sometimes outside my house there are lots of crowds
In my back garden there is a bright pink pool.

Zaini Miraj (12)
St James' CE Secondary School, Farnworth

Lions' Habitat

There's long grass,
Where they hide under,
With great mass,
When they strike it's like thunder,
There's unbearable heat,
You can't see them at night,
But their eyes are glowing,
As they're in their territory eating meat,
In their kingdom they're a fright,
And the habitat is good for not showing.

Krishan Tailor (12)
St James' CE Secondary School, Farnworth

Haiku

My house is unique
It is not always the same
It fills me with joy.

Jakub Amin (11)
St James' CE Secondary School, Farnworth

Home - Haiku

Comforted with snug,
My parents they comfort me,
Warm with happiness.

Louie Halliwell (11)
St James' CE Secondary School, Farnworth

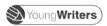

House In The River

Down in the river,
The little fish swim
And the eels slither
In the light that's dim,
It's nearly night-time
So the fish go to hide,
As the fishermen leave
With the fish names that rhyme,
In the bottom there's a hole that's wide,
Something's in there you wouldn't believe.

Sophie Middleton (12)
St James' CE Secondary School, Farnworth

Ode To Home

I share my home with others,
Others just like me.
Children, uncles, sisters, brothers,
It's nice, as they'd agree.
Our home has three floors,
It's like a huge cafeteria,
The kids are always nutty,
We live each in separate pores.
For I am of course bacteria,
Living in a bacon butty.

Ben Fennell (12)
St James' CE Secondary School, Farnworth

A Poem On My House

My house is very nice
It is also very special
But it does not have mice
And it has got a kettle
My house is nice and warm
My house is very big
My house is nice and bright
And it also has a lawn
But we hardly ever dig
And it has a very good sight.

Taybah Hassan (12)
St James' CE Secondary School, Farnworth

Owls

It's empty all night
And full all day
They hunt at night
They hide in the hay
Their favourite food is mouse
For the little baby
It has to be cosy
It's like a huge house
It's safe, maybe homely
Out of the way of the nosy.

Luke Thurston (12)
St James' CE Secondary School, Farnworth

Ode To Home

The home stands waiting
Calm and still
Quietly anticipating
Until . . .
The mantle clock bursts into life
The dog greets us at home.
Dad returns home from his daily strife
And the dog is rewarded his weekly bone
So we are both at home
Leave us alone.

Helen Sulkey (12)
St James' CE Secondary School, Farnworth

Ode To Home

My home is big, deep and blue,
I have lots of friends, colourful and bright,
I wonder if I can give you a clue,
One of my friends can show you the way with their light,
You might not know what I might be,
Swimming around in the sea,
My tail goes swish,
Do you know what I might be?
Me and my friends are in the sea,
Guess what, I'm a fish!

Firdose Valli (12)
St James' CE Secondary School, Farnworth

My House

As you walk into my house,
You will see paintings and photos and much more,
In my house you will definitely not see a mouse,
If you look to the left you'll see a big door,
And if you look a bit further you will see a lot more,
You are able to see the kitchen and the stairs,
And on the right is the games room,
Go back and go through the door,
And now it's time to go upstairs,
To look out that window and see the beautiful moon.

Dhylan Jadwa (12)
St James' CE Secondary School, Farnworth

Great Home - Haikus

Home is magical,
It is cosy yet playful,
At night it's peaceful.

Home you catch my eye,
I'll be with you till I die,
Swear I'll never lie.

Home you are evil,
You are worse than the devil
Oh I hate you home.

Rayan Saleh (12)
St James' CE Secondary School, Farnworth

Haiku Poems

I don't have a home,
I live on the dusty streets,
With no one to love.

My home is cosy,
It's filled with love, happiness,
Lovely peace to share!

My house is massive,
It's got enormous rooms and . . .
A big garden too!

Jasmine Patel (11)
St James' CE Secondary School, Farnworth

Warm, Cosy, Happy - Haiku

My house makes me feel
relaxed, snuggly and safe
and happy and fun!

Holly Leece (11)
St James' CE Secondary School, Farnworth

Home - Haiku

In bed with a ted
Surrounded with a blanket
So peaceful and warm.

Robyn Boyden (11)
St James' CE Secondary School, Farnworth

Homely - Haikus

My home is quite loud.
It is bursting with anger.
Sometimes it is fun.

I am a rich king.
I live in a big palace.
I rule the whole land.

I live in a shell.
I am slower than a slug.
I can be slimy.

Bradley Thorpe (11)
St James' CE Secondary School, Farnworth

Home - Haiku

I'm warm and cosy,
I am safe and protected,
I'm happy at home.

Jade Hayden (11)
St James' CE Secondary School, Farnworth

Homes

Homes, happiness, friends,
Others are less fortunate
Sadness, depression.

Aidan Smith (11)
St James' CE Secondary School, Farnworth

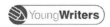

Paradise? - Haikus

My home, paradise
A safe haven where I rest
Personally mine

The homeless on streets
Outcast with no safe haven
Damp and unpleasant

My own golden shrine
Golden mahogany downstairs
Melted chocolate pool.

Ryan Newman (11)
St James' CE Secondary School, Farnworth

Abdul's Amazing Home - Haikus

I looked at my house,
In my house it's really huge,
Is this a sweet home?

Annoying sisters,
Makes me go really crazy,
They make a huge fight.

Is this a sweet home?
Inside I feel horrible,
They are horrible.

Abdul Aleem (11)
St James' CE Secondary School, Farnworth

Rich And Poor - Haikus

Mahogany wood,
My couch is as hot as fire,
My window is white.

Cardboard box is bed,
In the night I am freezing
And I have no socks.

I've a golden bed,
I've a flying car that glows
And my room is cool.

Vishaal Parmar (11)
St James' CE Secondary School, Farnworth

Tree House! - Haikus

My secret tree house,
That no one knows about and,
It is really cool.

My secret tree house,
It fills my heart with love and,
Keeps me nice and warm.

My secret tree house,
Mine to keep and never share,
That's my secret home!

Megan Brooks (11)
St James' CE Secondary School, Farnworth

Home

My room is my palace
And my home of what I want,
So why do I love my room
Because I am always on the hunt,
One side is wonders, one side is hobbies and what I love
Starting from the PS3 to wonderful books and DVDs
A giant TV and a giant fridge full of gorgeous food
After all I love my room because of my wonderful
Books, DVDs, PS3, giant fridge and TV!

Alireza Mafie (13)
St James' CE Secondary School, Farnworth

My Home

My house is nice and big
We all have lots of fun
My dog loves to dig
And we all love to sit in the sun
I love my family lots
They are so great to me
They're better than Jelly Tots
They love me that much
They always make my tea.

Ellise Gillard (12)
St James' CE Secondary School, Farnworth

My Home

Out of my shell
Into the big wide world
My friends say it's Hell
But most of them are girls

Slithering across the floor
And over the dome
When I get really slow
It's time to go back home.

Adam Walker (12)
St James' CE Secondary School, Farnworth

Home Sweet Home - Haiku

Rusty and nasty,
I live on the dirty streets,
I'm hungry all day.

Anita Vekaira (11)
St James' CE Secondary School, Farnworth

Home - Haiku

Home is delightful,
It gives me a warm feeling,
What a nice warm home!

Lisa Banks (12)
St James' CE Secondary School, Farnworth

Ode To Home

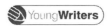

I watch him scurry on the sand
To find a house that's second-hand.
He crawls into a stray Coke can,
And stays because it has a fitted in fan.
Heavy it is on his back
Yet protecting him from all attack.
He does not ever like to share
This protects him from being a pair.

Patrick Kelly (12)
St James' CE Secondary School, Farnworth

An Ode To Home

A home is a place where you feel welcome,
A place where you fit in,
Somewhere that is comfy and somewhere you can relax
And do whatever you like to,
It's somewhere you can keep warm,
A place where you can sleep at night,
If all these things are possible
Then your house is a home.

Joshua Worswick (12)
St James' CE Secondary School, Farnworth

Ode To Home

Home is a comfortable place for me
Home is a great, warm and safe place for me.
When I am in my house
I'm never scared about those around me or the neighbours.
Whenever I go on holiday I miss my house a lot.
Then when I come home from holiday
It's lovely to be in my home sweet home.

Mitul Pankhania (12)
St James' CE Secondary School, Farnworth

Chloe's Home

I live in a house
It's normal size
I have a pet mouse
I never tell lies
My room is cool
Mine's the best
I have a pool
I am cooler than the rest!

Chloe Fairclough (12)
St James' CE Secondary School, Farnworth

Ode To Home

My home is cosy and warm
It makes me feel safe
My bedroom is gold and red
And I like my bed.
My home is big and beautiful
It makes me feel small.

Aaron Robinson (12)
St James' CE Secondary School, Farnworth

My Haikus About Home

The best thing at home,
Family supporting me,
I can't wish for more.

The freshness of home,
Makes me feel very grateful,
Lots of memories.

Hamza Rana (11)
St James' CE Secondary School, Farnworth

Ode To Home

My perfect home would be a mansion, the size of a castle.
There would be lots of rooms within this mansion.
My favourite room would be the games room
With all my gaming machines.
I would have a garden the size of a field,
Where I could ride bikes all day long.
And I would have many servants
Who would tend to my needs.

Brandon Topp (12)
St James' CE Secondary School, Farnworth

Creepy-Crawlies! - Haikus

All over the place
Creepy-crawlies in my house
Crawling all around!

Come and say hello
To my slimy hairy friends
Always around you!

Daniel Worthington (11)
St James' CE Secondary School, Farnworth

Home Sweet Home - Haikus

On thc strcct I live,
Freezing cold, dusty and wet
On the street I live . . .

My house is a dream
It's as tall as a tower,
And has twenty rooms.

Abigail Heywood (11)
St James' CE Secondary School, Farnworth

Heaven - Haikus

I was in Heaven.
Where I saw white bright flowers
Everything turned white.

My home was a cave
Where a dragon was talking
I was petrified.

Dhruv Chevli (11)
St James' CE Secondary School, Farnworth

Untitled

A home is cool
A home is nice
At home you will sit
A home is hot
A home is comfy
A home is somewhere you can party!

Matthew Cottam
St James' CE Secondary School, Farnworth

Home Sweet Home

Home sweet home, warm home.
Home sweet home, my peaceful home.
Home sweet home, my home.
Home is sweet 'cause it's peaceful.
Home is warm and mine.
My house is my home.

Bilaal Khan (11)
St James' CE Secondary School, Farnworth

My Pink World

I live in a pink posh house,
With a pink posh poodle,
Pretty birds singing,
All in a pretty pink tree,
Watched by my pretty pink cat,
Oh, if only my life was full of pink!

Emilia Singh (11)
St James' CE Secondary School, Farnworth

Home - Haiku

Ah I love my home
It may not be that perfect
There's no place like home.

Alisha Bond (11)
St James' CE Secondary School, Farnworth

Home - Haiku

Home is the sweetest
Comfy sofas and cushions
I have a good home.

Ahmed Chohan (11)
St James' CE Secondary School, Farnworth

All Alone

Bleak and desolate,
I'm here, *only* me, alone,
Lonely and quiet.

Zahra Khan (11)
St James' CE Secondary School, Farnworth

Home - Haiku

My house is cosy,
I'm in a semi-detached,
And I'm quite relaxed.

Charlotte Turner (11)
St James' CE Secondary School, Farnworth

Home

I always feel safe
It is the place I love most,
I'm a lucky boy.

Chris German (11)
St James' CE Secondary School, Farnworth

Home - Haiku

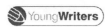

I live in a house,
Where I am comfortable,
I can just let go.

Rachel Hayes (11)
St James' CE Secondary School, Farnworth

My House - Haiku

My house is quite big
I feel safe with family
I am loved at home!

Jacob Swaries (12)
St James' CE Secondary School, Farnworth

My Home - Haiku

My home is special
It is full of memories
That's my special place.

Sameer Patel (11)
St James' CE Secondary School, Farnworth

Haiku

This is my great home,
My comfortable safe home,
My house is the best.

Uvais Malji (11)
St James' CE Secondary School, Farnworth

Ode To House - Haiku

My home is a shed
At home I play the Xbox
And lie on my bed.

Daniel Hulmes (12)
St James' CE Secondary School, Farnworth

My Home - Haiku

My home is haunted,
Ghosts wail loudly and shrilly
Gliding and swooping.

Husain Patel (11)
St James' CE Secondary School, Farnworth

Haiku

Bang-bang! What's that noise?
I'm sure I packed all my toys,
Oh, you tricked me boys.

Corben Davies (11)
St James' CE Secondary School, Farnworth

Home Sweet Home - Haiku

A sweet home with a
Lovely, caring family
It makes me happy!

Unaisah Patel (11)
St James' CE Secondary School, Farnworth

Crackers? - Haiku

Squirrels live in trees.
If they fall they'll hurt their knees.
They get nuts and keys.

Corben John Davies (11)
St James' CE Secondary School, Farnworth

Haiku

Family all round
Safe, secure, warm and cosy
Grateful where I live.

Jamil Noorgat (11)
St James' CE Secondary School, Farnworth

Haiku

My beautiful home
Is as beautiful as a
Massive butterfly.

Jake Taylor (11)
St James' CE Secondary School, Farnworth

Home - Haiku

I love my good home,
It is the best home ever,
It is nice and calm.

Victoria Unwin (11)
St James' CE Secondary School, Farnworth

The Jungle's Creatures

The jungle closes her leafy arms in,
Hiding the exotic creatures that lie within.
Some wide, some large, some very small,
Some walk, some fly, some slither, some crawl.

Sooty panthers shoot out of the grass like a whizzing bullet,
Their stealthy claws are sharper than the scales of a mullet,
Orange chimpanzees swing in the towering trees,
Reaching out their arms and extending their knees.

An angry lion's roar shakes the delicate ground,
The treetops tremble and quiver with the tremendous sound.
Vividly dressed flowers sway and show their petals,
While butterflies and insects, on their buds comfortably settle.

Long entwining grass grows up from beneath,
Sharp and glistening like razor-sharp teeth.
Ruby-eyed bats are smothered in grey,
As they fly screeching, reaching towards their helpless prey.

The giraffes' brown dotty necks extend very long,
As they nibble at juicy leaves with their long slimy tongues.
Venus fly traps soar up many centimetres high,
They smile beneath their buds as they gobble up a fly.

The jungle's rain is pouring and pounding down,
Clothing the smooth grass in a raindrop silk gown.
All the animals in this jungle, every sweet furry face,
Shall live for now peacefully in this beautiful, exotic place.

But in the future some time, some other day,
This beautiful place may be a different way.
Just bare land, no trees, no animals, no habitat,
For if we don't act now it could be just like that.
Because of us - humans - destroying their home to make more money, more room.
Can't we see our selfishness will lead to their doom?

Abigail Blood (11)
Summerhill Secondary School, Kingswinford

Growing

At one a little child was she,
Young and innocent and unable to read,

Yet she quickly grew to zero and three,
And we became friends: her and me.

At zero and nine,
She promised that I would be fine,

But by ten and five,
I was to stay behind,

Yet soon she grew to twenty and eight,
And decided perhaps it wasn't too late.

So by twenty and nine,
Her beauty was mine,

This is why by the time she grew to thirty and three,
We have five children, a house and an orchard of trees,

At forty and five,
She laughed and she'd cried,

At fifty and seven,
Her life felt like heaven,

At sixty and two,
She was shocked at how time flew,

At eighty and nine,
Her health remained fine,

At ninety and two
She said goodbye to you,

Till at last, I did bid her goodnight and goodbye,
And said I would love her till the moment she died.

Matilda Lloyd Williams (12)
The Queen's School, Chester

Burning The Past

Collect all the leaves up,
Mound after mound.
Strike a match and light them,
Burn them to the ground.

Get rid of all the memories,
Get rid of all the past.
Destroy all the evidence,
Burn them, do it fast.

It's time to move on,
It's time to forget.
Leave our sadness behind,
But this isn't over yet.

End it now, end it quick,
Before it's too late.
Burn the anger, burn the fear,
Take away the hate.

Collect all the leaves up,
Mound after mound.
Strike a match and light them,
Burn them to the ground.

Jessica Reed (13)
The Queen's School, Chester

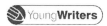

Separated Lovers

The moon cries his sorrow to everyone,
Calling to his lost love, the sun

Who waited so long in their meeting place,
But then gave up and turned her face

The night, so black in her mourning clothes,
Grieves for the day, but the moon knows

The sun is not gone, she's somewhere near,
And in a while she'll reappear

However, these lovers can never join,
A silver penny and a golden coin

And though they drag their weary feet,
Towards each other, they never meet

For when the sun lights up the sky,
The moon, he fades with an angry cry

The sun and moon will never be together,
They cannot touch, separated forever.

Bethany Reed (13)
The Queen's School, Chester

Broken

The waves of sound crashed against the sordid form
A heart beats out an ominous rhythm
Echoing the sound she once made
By home's loving care.
That pulse: seeping red cascades into blue
That reminder, that ache, that sorrow
A broken home, a broken heart.

The darkness creeps in with every pound
Streaming into the veins of the house
Drowning in the darkest blood.
The half-light screams at her
That reminder, that ache, that sorrow
A broken home, a broken heart.

And then a scent engulfs her
The tantalising smell of the ocean;
Salt air dances through her senses
Taunting her body.
That beautiful memory
That reminder, that ache, that sorrow
A broken home, a broken heart.

And now the rhythm fades
The heart struggles, then falters
The house breathes for the last
Then silence.
A vestige of the thoughts that once it had
Perish with the half-light.
But the pain resides within
That reminder, that ache, that sorrow
That broken home, this broken heart.

Claire Lightfoot
Upton Hall School, Wirral

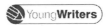

Broken

Pitter-patter, pitter-patter
The sound of the rain
Like the tears that used to fall
Careering down broken windows and broken homes

The fiery smell of whiskey
Spilt over an icy floor
The smell of our front room
Igniting the smell of fallacious love

A slamming door
Shattering fragile windows
Like our front door
Becoming a shield hiding a fractured home from a careless world

A pure black sky
Plain, without any luminous stars
And the clouds that cover up all our hope
Taking me back to my broken home once again.

Stephanie Addenbrooke (15)
Upton Hall School, Wirral

Home

In the deep silence of the night
The groan of an old wooden floorboard takes me back.
It takes me back home, back to a life of warmth, love and light.
But I cannot return to that life, it is gone.
I must suffer the torture of a cold, dark world filled with hatred.

The moon lights up a dull black sky.
No stars, no light, besides the ever watching moon.
Queen of the night sky.
In the darkness the world becomes a different place.
A sinister place enclosing me in its darkness.

The light smell of the air on a brisk autumn morning reminds me of home.
It reminds me of the life I had before.
As the autumn breeze blows I feel as if it takes my troubles away.
But the wind can't, no one can.
No one can ever take my troubles away.

Home. It feels like a lifetime ago.
Familiar sounds and comforting smells,
They will stay with me forever.
Just like the memories I hold close to my heart.
But dread fills my mind as I think of returning there.
Home.

Rebecca Airey
Upton Hall School, Wirral

Home

The piercing screech of a bewildered cat
Takes me back there
Back to a place of broken dreams,
Of hateful love.
Home.

I can see the dark shadows
Creeping along the floorboards,
Masking the whispered secrets within each corner.
Lies.

Suffocating breaths of home-made bread
Attempt to fill the cracks in our hearts,
But scars will not fade, they always lurk.
Forever.

That spiteful place is hard to bear
But all the same, it's home, I grew up there.

Amy Naylor
Upton Hall School, Wirral

Why Teenagers Love Drink

You see them on the park,
On a Friday night,
Vandalising and graffiti
Anything in their path.

With the big red eyes wobbling you,
As the alcohol kicks in,
So close the anger,
Picking a fight,
For their own right.

Forming gangs,
On streets near you.

Lewis Bolton (12)
Westleigh High School, Leigh

Stereotypes

Stereotypes are all that we see,
Teenage hooligans
Scattered in the news on TV.
Truth is we're not all the same,
Not there to cause trouble,
Or just to be a pain.
All we care for is alcohol and drugs,
Nothing else matters,
Cos every one of us are thugs.
The bad things always make good news,
They don't care about us,
About our feelings and views.

Thugs, chavs and yobs,
That's what you think we all are.
You think if you walk past us,
We'll steal the keys to your car.
Truth is we're not all bad,
Most of us do help and care,
Like helping an old lady cross the road
Till she is safely there.

The media infects everyone's brain
Into thinking us teenagers are
All the same.
99.9% of us are good,
We're not all thugs you know,
Just misunderstood.

Ashley Poole (14)
Westleigh High School, Leigh

Do Looks Really Matter?

Straighten the hair,
Put on the clothes,
Smooth out the make-up,
Texts on my phone.

Feeling alive,
Feeling good,
Looking better,
Than I ever could.

Ready to go,
Walk out the door,
The hair is a mess,
But I can't see to it anymore.

Lip gloss in bag,
Head held high,
Walking with swag,
Me and my crew.

McFly on the radio,
Blasting my music,
Singing songs from the stereo,
Headphones are in.

The life of me!

Georgia Fishburn (13)
Westleigh High School, Leigh

Nobody Cares

Crash! The sound of a child hitting the floor
Nobody cares,
Nobody will,
Face pouring,
Nose broken,
Nobody cares,
Nobody will.

The sorrow rages as people walk past,
Nobody cares, nobody will,
Lip cracked,
Face smashed,
Nobody cares,
Nobody will.

Bike in hand, crossing the road,
Blood still pouring,
Nobody lets him cross,
Nobody cares,
Nobody will.

He dies!
Painfully,
Nobody cares,
Nobody will.

Barney Warburton (13)
Westleigh High School, Leigh

Teenage Discrimination

Why do people think we're yobs
And because of that we can get no jobs
Everyone thinks we're always getting into trouble
It's like we're all living in our own little bubble
And at the end of the day it ends in tears and sobs

We're a forgotten breed, us teenage crowd
And some of us spit and swear and talk too loud
With parents ringing in our ears
Because we've gotten too cocky over the years
And they just want us to make them proud

We carry around guns and knives
But all we're doing is wasting lives
But we're not all the same
In fact, some of us want a bit of fame
And have celebrity wives

As young adults we should be treated with respect
And that's the least you would expect
So to conclude this poem
There's something you should be knowing
Us teenagers are alright
Even though we stand around in the night.

Nathan Murray (13)
Westleigh High School, Leigh

What Matters To Me?

Friends.
My lucky stars
They light up my life
When things get dark
That's what matters to me.

Boys.
Girls' fantasies
Young, fit, sweet and cute
Every girl's teenage dream
That's what matters to me.

School.
Work, life, GCSEs
Getting a fantastic job
That's what matters to me.

Life.
Work, friends, boys
To get through life
You have to make a choice
But that's what matters to me.

Alicia Lovely (13)
Westleigh High School, Leigh

Teenage Prejudice

Every day we face prejudice,
Accepting the strong and verbal hits,
Teenagers today are not as they seem,
We all have ambitions, hopes and dreams.

Chavs, hoodies, hooligans, yobs,
You think we're cocky with our big gobs.
Maybe if you get to know us teenagers,
You'll know we're not violent strangers.

We're courteous, happy, nice and polite,
We don't go out looking for a fight.
You think we just stand on corners with our beer,
Whilst you sit inside and tremble with fear.

So what do you think of us now?
Do you accept that we're calm and quiet
Or expect us to begin a riot?
It's up to you, you decide.

Chelsea Latter (14)
Westleigh High School, Leigh

Spotlights And Stages

Single spotlight
Centre-stage
Break a leg
Curtains fade

Playing a different personality
Being a person you want to be
A sensation of feeling free
Show's begun, now watch me

Laughs arise
Tears flow
Comedy or drama
Just give it a go

Playing a different personality
Being a person you want to be
A sensation of feeling free
Lights go down, one, two, three.

Charlotte Durham (13)
Westleigh High School, Leigh

My Life

Will my life be just as good growing up in the neighbourhood?
Will I be rich or will I be poor?
If I want to be rich, I will have to know a lot more.
If I don't want to be poor I'll have to get a lot of money to make sure.
I will take care of my family because they matter to me,
So I can try to make them happy like me.
Mum, Dad, Brother are family,
We all try to be happy wherever we are.
I have a dog called Bruno who's one year but also like a peer.

Nathan Pittendrigh (12)
Westleigh High School, Leigh

I'm Now A Teenager

It's my birthday,
Thirteen today,
I'm now a teenager,
Hip hip hooray!

I walk round the block,
Head in the sky,
I'm now a teenager,
Hopes up high.

I go on the park,
Too cool for swings,
I'm now a teenager,
I need to try other things.

It was my birthday,
Thirteen yesterday,
I am now a teenager,
The excitement's over today.

Hayley Masheder (13)
Westleigh High School, Leigh

The Heroes In Afghanistan

We have to stay strong, for our heroes out in Afghanistan.
We wait for letters and phone calls to see how they are.
When we don't get one we worry and wonder
But we are really proud of them.

They fight for our country but they don't ask for help,
So support the heroes
And wish for them to come home safe and sound.

Sophie Bretherton (13)
Westleigh High School, Leigh

My Bully

My bully has short, spiky hair,
His eyes are as red as fire,
He only has six teeth and even they are black,
But don't worry, I'll tell the teacher.

He has a broad body that makes him look bionic,
With his super strength and never-ending stamina,
He plans to beat me up,
But don't worry I'll tell the teacher.

As I walk to the head teacher's door I realise he is behind me,
He has long legs, so if I run he'll easily catch me,
I turn to face him and say,
'I'm not worried, I'll tell the head teacher.'

As I tell the head teacher I feel relieved,
A week has passed and no signs of him,
What happened? Expelled? Excluded?
Who cares, I told the teacher.

Adam Cachia (13)
Westleigh High School, Leigh

I'm Scared

I am scared of what will happen to my family and friends.
Will the world ever end?
Just like silver, just like gold
There's always a secret never to be told.

Abbie O'Neil (12)
Westleigh High School, Leigh

Why Bully?

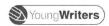

Why bully?
Calling in school,
Pushing me, hitting me,
Why bully?

Weekends,
They wait for me,
Throw things at my window,
I can't leave the house,
Why bully?

I'm scared of going outside,
I walk to my friend's house.
They circle me,
My clothes are ripped.

Why me?
Why bully?

Callum Barber (12)
Westleigh High School, Leigh

Friendships

Some friendships sail away into the night sky.
But that's only when the fire dies.
But not all friendships end like this.
All it might need is a small kiss.
When a best friend becomes a lover.

You may laugh together. Giggle together,
Cry together and sigh together.
That's simply because they've got your back,
And wouldn't change or swap you for the world.

Rachel Alice Gregory (12)
Westleigh High School, Leigh

What Will I Do?

What does the future hold?
At school I do as I am told,
But there will come a time
Where the choice will be mine.
What will I do?

My future worries me,
I really wish I could see
What the future holds for me,
I don't know what to be,
What will I do?

I could be a game designer,
But could end up in a diner.
The future seems like a test,
The thing to do is try my best,
What will I do?

Connor Sharratt (13)
Westleigh High School, Leigh

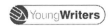

The Pathway

This is the time,
Our hearts pounding,
Our heads sweating,
Our brains stressing.

This is it,
Now is the time,
The time to choose,
Our pathways
To our future.

And now we decide,
Moments pass,
Pens down,
And that is it,
Our future is chosen,
Our pathway has started.

Joy Burns (13)
Westleigh High School, Leigh

No Money Or Jobs

Too many people losing their jobs.
Too many people with no money.
Too many people trying to get into college.
Too many people can't afford college.
How many years will this go on?

Not enough jobs.
Not enough money.
Not enough colleges.
Not enough universities.
Will there be enough for me?

No jobs.
No money.
No college.
This is what worries me.

Rebecca Cotterell (12)
Westleigh High School, Leigh

My Pain

Rejected by all the people around you,
No sense of security or understanding.
Unable to think about a homely future,
Unable to think about any future.

Lonely, pushed and shoved because of who you are,
Kicked and bruised because of the way you look.
Why do you let them do it to you?
Why do you absorb all of the pain, anger, confusion and bottle it up?
Is it because you know of the consequences?
That no one will believe you, no one.

Scared, writhing in panic, thinking he's behind again,
Trying to show no fear in your eyes.
You wonder why one person should suffer so much to this extent.
Rejected, lonely, scared, I never thought it would go this far.

Dillon Swanton (14)
Westleigh High School, Leigh

Afghanistan

We need to believe that they will be OK
And stay strong for our country.
You wait for letters and phone calls to come home.

They could come home any time,
When we don't get a phone call home
We want to know what's going on.
When they come back home you get love and kisses.

Jordan Hellam (12)
Westleigh High School, Leigh

Gangster Life!

Gangsters are mean, brutal and tough,
Driving around smashing stuff.
Buying drugs and dealing things,
Always doing the wrong thing.
They think they're big and clever
But I'd never mess with them.

Gangsters love to wear baggy pants,
Riding around as though people are ants.
Bullying people they don't know,
Never take the answer no.
Swiping shiny and expensive things,
Nicking diamonds and ruby rings.

Robbing, stealing and lying is never any good,
Unless you want to end up face first in the mud.

Lewis Grimes (12)
Westleigh High School, Leigh

Young Writers Information

We hope you have enjoyed reading this book - and that you will continue to enjoy it in the coming years.

If you like reading and writing poetry drop us a line, or give us a call, and we'll send you a free information pack.

Alternatively if you would like to order further copies of this book or any of our other titles, then please give us a call or log onto our website at www.youngwriters.co.uk

Young Writers Information
Remus House
Coltsfoot Drive
Peterborough
PE2 9BF
(01733) 890066